Teammate Tuesdays

Volume III

Another Year of Good Teammate Musings

LANCE LOYA

CAGER HAUS
PUBLISHING

ISBN-13: 978-1-7325505-7-5

www.coachloya.com

Design and publishing by Cager Haus.
Cover image by Kutsal Lenger, Dreamstime.com.

For Laken and Lakota…may you always be good teammates.

Contents

Acknowledgements

A special thank you to Wendy Clouner for suggesting that I start a blog. Although I wasn't initially receptive to your suggestion, I am glad I eventually acquiesced. I also want to express my gratitude to Rachel Loya, Cindy Davis, Jerry Pirrung, and Craig Sikurinec for your continued support and recommendations.

I would also like the thank my Good Teammate Factory clients and the online community members who read blogs, like and share posts, and offer invaluable feedback and encouragement. They are the fuel that powers the *Be a Good Teammate* movement.

Introduction

Welcome to *Teammate Tuesdays Volume III!* Assembling a third book of this nature is a little surreal to me, as is how this book series came to be.

Once upon a time, I set out on a journey to discover an answer to the question: What does it *really* mean to be a good teammate? Everybody belongs to some type of team. Maybe it's an actual sports team, or maybe it's the place where you work, the community you live in, the church you attend, or simply your family. Ultimately, the success of any team depends on its members' capacity to be good teammates. But what specifically does *being a good teammate* mean?

My journey of discovery began with the publication of a children's book called *Be a Good Teammate.* The book revolved around the idea that good teammates do three things: care, share, and listen. I wrote it with the sole intention of conveying some fatherly advice to my daughters, who were learning to read.

But *Be a Good Teammate* unexpectedly set into motion a sequence of events that changed the trajectory of my life and led to the realization that the world needs more good teammates—kind, mindful, unselfish individuals who put the needs of their "teams" ahead of their own agendas. It's a belief that transcends sports and applies to all varieties of teams.

The journey eventually brought me to a point where exploring the art of being a good teammate became my life's work. Somewhere along the way, I decided to heed the advice of a trusted friend and share my discoveries—my *musings*—through a weekly blog. I called the blog "Teammate Tuesdays," and every Tuesday morning I posted a new entry.

As the blog's following grew, subscribers began reaching out to me about the possibility of making the content available in print form. They wanted to give the blog as a gift to their friends, families, and teammates. To accommodate the recurring requests, I turned the entire first year of my blog into a book titled *Teammate Tuesdays: A Year of Good Teammate Musings*.

The book you're presently reading is a compilation of the entire third year of my blog. Like the previous volumes, this book will provide you with an abundance of "good teammate" stories, observations, and insights—each capable of transforming you into a better teammate.

The year covered in this volume proved to be more personally eventful than the previous volumes. In some ways, it was a year of losses for me. I lost my sister to cancer. I lost my father to Alzheimer's. I even lost one of my organs to gallbladder disease. My *losses* became sources of inspiration and are discussed in the pages that follow.

In other ways, it was a year of gains for me. I gained a deeper understanding and appreciation for the art of being a good teammate. I also gained a new book—in addition to this one. In mid-November, I finally released *The WE Gear: How Good Teammates Shift from Me to We*, a book I started writing before I launched my blog. Some of the concepts introduced in *The WE Gear* are mentioned in this book.

Perhaps most noteworthy for this volume, though, was the arrival of the COVID-19 virus. The final five chapters were influenced by the emergence of terms like social distancing, quarantine, and pandemic. Ironically, the global COVID-19 situation provided meaningful "good teammate" insight.

It's worth noting that this book is written in a more informal, conversational tone—the way blogs typically are. Each post (chapter) was written as an independent entity. With a few exceptions, like the removal of embedded hyperlinks, the posts weren't altered from how they originally appeared online. Sometimes this translates into me repeating a particular word or phrase in consecutive chapters. An editor wouldn't allow this to happen in a traditional book. But I suspect it won't take much effort on your part to see past this type of minor faux pas and still appreciate the lesson.

I like the idea of assembling an entire year's worth of posts in a book format. The posts are worth sharing in an alternative medium. Not everyone who can benefit from the message reads online blogs. Some people still prefer to hold a physical book in their hands. Putting the blog in book form makes it possible to share the message with a broader audience.

A book is also a convenient way to bring up to speed those who may be joining the Good Teammate movement *already in progress*. The format allows you to experience your own journey of discovery, at your own pace. You don't have to wait until next week to find out what I am going to write about in my blog. You can read the posts as fast or slow as you desire. It's like binge watching a blog.

I am asked two common questions: *Why Tuesdays?* and *Why doesn't the first chapter start on January 1?*

We all have seasons to our lives. For some, it's spring, summer, fall, and winter. For those involved in sports, it's preseason, regular season, postseason, and offseason. I wrote my first blog post at the end of April, coinciding with what was at that time considered to be the start of my offseason— the ideal time to start new endeavors. I have consistently added a new post every week since then.

Why Tuesdays? I am a fan of Mitch Albom's memoir *Tuesday's with Morrie*. In the book, he chronicles the wisdom acquired from his weekly visits with his former sociology professor Morrie Swartz, who is dying from ALS. The name *Teammate Tuesdays* was a tip of the hat of sorts to Albom's book and its touching premise. But that's not the only reason. I also believe that Tuesdays are generally the best days for personal and professional development.

Wednesdays mark the middle of the week. It's *hump day*. You've come to the realization that you better put your nose to the grindstone and get busy or you're going to run out of time.

Thursdays still have some of the same urgency to get your work done as Wednesdays. But by Thursday afternoon, you are starting to set your sights on the weekend.

Fridays are the day to wrap up loose ends and then coast through the rest of the day. It's the end of the work week, so you're reluctant to start any new projects. You may also feel burned out by Friday and not necessarily motivated to engage in anything mentally taxing.

Saturdays are spent catching up on chores, like cutting grass and doing laundry. Saturdays are additionally a day for recreation and seeking fun.

Sundays are family time. You're ready to relax and spend quality time with your family. If you're struggling with your job, you'll probably spend Sunday evening stressing about having to go back to work the next day. Professional development isn't a high priority on Sundays.

Mondays are consumed with playing catch up. You're trying to finish all the work you didn't complete—but should have—last week. You're also being bombarded with everything that was delivered over the weekend. You seem to have an endless amount of pressing emails and phone calls to return. By the time Mondays are over, you are exhausted.

Which brings us to Tuesdays. You are tired from playing catch up on Monday and not anxious to put in another intense day of work. You also manage to convince yourself that you still have the rest of the week to get your work done.

Why start today? Tuesdays are the perfect day to invest in self-improvement.

Sound familiar? If so, then you've come to the right place. Every day is Tuesday in this book.

I hope you enjoy my collection of good teammate musings. My wish is for them to inspire you to become a better version of yourself and to equip you to help others do the same.

Come to Work Day
APRIL 30

Twenty-six years ago, a group of New York City educators reached out to the Ms. Foundation about a troubling pattern of behavior they had been noticing with young women in their schools.

The Ms. Foundation was involved in research that found young women's loss of self-esteem to be a primary reason for their making poor life choices and for their not doing well in school. In concert with child development experts and educators, Gloria Steinem, co-founder of *Ms.* magazine, launched a pilot program aimed at improving young women's self-esteem.

As part of the program, professional mentors asked participants a poignant question: "If you could grow up to be anything, what would it be?"

An article about Steinem's program subsequently appeared in *Parade Magazine* and led to the first ever "Take Our Daughters to Work Day." The event, now celebrated annually on the fourth Thursday of April, was expanded in 2002 to include young men and renamed "Take Our Daughters and Sons to Work Day."

I love the premise of the occasion. It's more than a career day or even job shadowing. Take Our Daughters and Sons to Work Day is an opportunity to share and inspire. It's an opportunity to impact the future.

I wanted my daughter Laken, a fourth grader, to experience Take Your Daughters and Sons to Work Day. For an entrepreneur, however, taking my daughter "to work" was a little challenging. I didn't necessarily have a specific work place to take her, so I improvised.

Since I wasn't scheduled to speak at any events on that day, I decided to let my daughter assist in writing this week's blog. The two of us sat in a Starbucks—where I typically write most of my blogs—sipped our respective beverages and typed away on my laptop. We went through the entire process of how my blog starts with an idea, gets refined through online research, written, posted to the backend of my website, and ultimately ends up as a chapter in a book.

It was a mutually memorable experience.

The Take Our Daughters and Sons to Work Day website listed some recommended activities to help facilitate a meaningful day for the participants. We incorporated part of one of those activities into what we wrote.

The activity was called "When You Were My Age" and revolved around the child interviewing the parent. I agreed to let my daughter pick two questions from the list to ask me, in exchange for her agreeing to answer two questions from me about being a good teammate—a bit of *quid pro quo*, if you will.

(*In an effort to capture the authenticity of my daughter's responses, I chose to not correct her spelling, grammar, or sentence structure. I left everything exactly as she wrote it.)

LAKEN: Did you follow your original career path?

ME: No. When I was your age, I wanted to be a professional athlete. That's the path I started on, but that's not where my journey took me. I never imagined I would be doing what I currently do. I didn't like reading and I had a bad speech impediment when I was your age, so becoming an author who gives speeches wasn't the direction I would've expected my career to take. But that's what makes life so amazing, we never know what surprises await us. Everything that happens to us is part of the adventure and prepares us for the next stage in our journey. I love what I do for a living and wouldn't have it any other way.

LAKEN: Who helped you make your career dision?

ME: I had several incredible teachers and coaches who had an impact on my life. They all influenced my career choices, and I am grateful to them more than they will ever know. But...YOU are the one who helped me make my career decision! I wanted you to have a better life and for you to be equipped with the skills to make the world a better place. You are the one who inspired me to write *Be a Good Teammate* and pursue a new a career. Every decision I make in my career is influenced by you.

Now it was my turn…

ME: Why is being a good teammate important?

LAKEN: It is important to be a good teammate because if there were not good teammates in the world everyone would argue. People wouldn't share their knowledge, so some people wouldn't be able to get an educashun. People also wouldn't listen to others, so nobody would understand each other's problems. Finally, no one would care about anything and the world wouldn't be happy.

ME: How can you get others to be good teammates?

LAKEN: You can get others to be good teammates by spreading the word about it and by doing the teammate actions (which are care, share, and listen). You can set a good example. When you see someone make a good teammate move, you can recanaze it. You can encorige them to continue doing that. They will realize how it feels to have a good teammate help them, which will cause a chain effect to being a good teammate.

Isn't it enlightening to step back and see a complex world through the eyes of a child? Adults tend to overcomplicate problems, but children seldom do. I made a point to not influence my daughter's answers and to let her replies be genuine. And I think they were.

I continuously emphasize the importance of being a good teammate to her, but it's still emotionally moving to discover how much she has absorbed.

You may have noticed that the name of the event is Take *our* Daughters and Sons to Work Day; not Take *my* Daughter and Son to Work Day. The event takes a village/team approach. Any parent or grandparent or aunt or uncle or mentor who unselfishly shares the experiences of his or her life with a child influences the future in a positive way.

The good teammate lesson to be learned from all of this is that the future of the team always matters to good teammates. Good teammates are committed to perpetuating the team's success and that means having a willingness to share themselves with the younger members of their teams.

This is true on sports teams, corporate teams, and life teams.

As always…Good teammates care. Good teammates share. Good teammates listen. Go be a good teammate.

Nice Guys Are the Only Ones Who Finish
MAY 7

The label "nice guy" carries an undeserved stigma in sports. In *Building Good Teammates*, I wrote: "Whoever said nice guys finish last was too impatient. In the end, nice guys are the only ones who finish."

A man named Leo "The Lip" Durocher is the *whoever* credited with coining the expression "Nice guys finish last." Durocher was an outspoken baseball player and coach. He played with Babe Ruth on the New York Yankees team that won the 1928 World Series.

But a strained relationship with the team's ownership led to the fiery infielder being traded to the Cincinnati Reds the following season. He bounced around several other teams before eventually becoming the player/coach of the Brooklyn Dodgers.

In *42*, the film about Jackie Robinson breaking major league baseball's color barrier, actor Christopher Meloni, of Law & Order SVU fame, portrayed Durocher.

"Nice guys finish last" was a condensed version of what Durocher actually said. When asked about the cordial nature of the New York Giants, the Dodger's crosstown rivals, he replied, "The nice guys are all over there, in seventh place." At the time, seventh place was next to last place in the league. Journalists shortened the headline to "Nice Guys' Wind Up in Last Place, Scoffs Lippy."

Durocher shortened the quote ever further when he titled his 1975 autobiography *Nice Guys Finish Last*. The idea has evolved to imply a correlation between being nice and finishing last—i.e. failure. But that is simply not true. You can be a decent person and succeed.

Nice guys are friendly, gracious, unselfish, kind, thoughtful, and considerate. Good teammates embody those same qualities. Good teammates are *nice guys*. No team sustains success without having good teammates. In other words, no team sustains success without having nice guys.

The caring, unselfish nature of a good teammate is the reason teams succeed. They have a willingness to sacrifice for the betterment of their team. Sure, you can get ahead, at least temporarily, without being nice.

Cheating, behaving unethically, or acting dishonestly may gain you an advantage. Speaking harshly and treating others poorly may produce momentary results. "Un-nice" behavior may help you win a game, or even a championship. But it won't help you win at life.

When those on their deathbeds reflect on their lives, they don't think about the games they won, or the championships they won, or any of the material possessions they acquired.

They measure their life by the meaningful relationships they formed, how well they treated others, and the positive differences they made in the world. The absence of those benchmarks makes it hard to consider a life to have successfully finished. In the end, nice guys *are* the only ones who finish.

Leo "The Lip" Durocher was elected to the Baseball Hall of Fame in 1994. He achieved considerable success as a player, and even more so as a coach. Ironically, Durocher was replaced as the Dodger's starting shortstop by a player named Pee Wee Reese, who famously stood in solidarity with Jackie Robinson and is considered to be one of the greatest teammates of all time.

Perhaps even more ironic is that in spite of all of Durocher's success on the baseball diamond, he is best remembered for the controversial support he gave Jackie Robinson. When Dodger's players began circulating a petition demanding Robinson be removed from the team, Durocher called a team meeting and told the players in no certain terms, "I don't care if he (Jackie Robinson) is yellow or black or has stripes like a [censored] zebra. I'm his manager and I say he plays." Only a *nice guy* would provide that level of support. In the end, Leo "The Lip" Durocher is indeed remembered for being nice.

As always…Good teammates care. Good teammates share. Good teammates listen. Go be a good teammate.

Details about Leo Durocher's life are from: "The Team That Forever Changed Baseball and America: The 1947 Brooklyn Dodgers" by Society for American Baseball Research (University of Nebraska Press, 2012).

Who's the Best GOT Teammate?
MAY 14

With Sunday night's airing of the series finale, HBO's *Game of Thrones* will officially come to an end. I have grown to become a "GOT" fan. I wasn't initially, but a friend's insistence that I "get on board" and start watching the show led to my present state of fandom.

I didn't get the hype at first. Is it about kings and queens? Dragons? Dwarfs? Zombies? Does it take place in the past or the future? Is it drama? Romance? Action-adventure? Science fiction?

I eventually came to understand that part of the show's appeal is that it is *sort of* all of those things. Like many of history's epic television shows, *Game of Thrones* breaks the mold and transcends genre limitations.

Last summer, I finally caved to the pressure and watched season one, episode one—which quickly turned into a *Game of Thrones* marathon. Over the next several days, I binge watched every episode of the first seven seasons, only to be left hanging, anxiously awaiting the arrival of this spring's eighth and final season.

I spend most of the time pondering the art of being a good teammate. With the final GOT episode looming, however, I've had an intermingling of thoughts taking place in my head. I've found myself wondering: *Who is the best Game of Thrones teammate?*

The show is entertaining and has lots of examples of great leadership. But what about flat out *good teammate-ness?* Who is the best "good teammate" on the show? After much consideration, I've narrowed my choices down to five possibilities, and I'm not prepared, nor capable, of taking it any further than that. I'll leave it up to you to make the final determination.

(*If you're not a Game of Thrones *fan, keep reading. You don't have to know the characters to appreciate their qualities. Even if you've never seen a single episode, you'll value the good teammate lesson that follows.)*

Jon Snow

Description from the official GOT website: Ned's bastard son. He joins the Night's Watch, following in the footsteps of his Uncle Benjen.

Qualifying characteristics: Jon is a man of action. When he comes across a problem, he confronts it. Even though he demonstrates strong leadership qualities, he never seeks individual glory. Jon is courageous and routinely stands up for those who cannot stand up for themselves. He chooses to do what is right and not necessarily what is popular.

Possible disqualifying characteristics: Sometimes Jon fails to recognize an issue's complexities. He oversimplifies problems and acts when he should show restraint. His lack of patience can put his team in vulnerable situations.

Brienne of Tarth

Description from the official GOT website: Brienne is a highborn lady who would rather be a knight. As Catelyn Stark's envoy, she is tasked with escorting Jaime Lannister back to King's Landing.

Qualifying characteristics: Brienne is fiercely loyal. She takes her commitment to serve seriously. Her motives are always pure, and she is trustworthy beyond measure.

Possible disqualifying characteristics: Brienne has a chip on her shoulder about being a female "knight." She's often distracted by what others think of her instead of being totally comfortable in her own skin. Her uneasiness is understandable, but her insecurities cause her to be a loner and not engage with other team members.

Tyrion Lannister

Description from the official GOT website: Called "The Imp," because of his small stature, he is the youngest son of Tywin Lannister, the richest lord in the Seven Kingdoms, and younger brother to Queen Cersei and Ser Jaime Lannister. What he lacks in height, he makes up in wit.

Qualifying characteristics: His team matters to him. He genuinely cares about the citizens of Westeros and those he serves. He's invested in their well-being. In a realm filled with combat, Tyrion's size restricts his ability to contribute on the battlefield. But he is an example of someone who embraces his role on the team and finds a way to alternatively use his gift—his intellect—to contribute to his team's success.

Possible disqualifying characteristics: Tyrion tends to overindulge in personal pleasures. He frequents brothels and drinks to excess. His character has improved over the course of the series but allowing overindulgences to be a detriment to the team is always cause for concern.

Podrick Payne

Description from the official GOT website: Quiet and unassuming, Podrick is Tyrion's squire.

Qualifying characteristics: He's a good listener and a loyal, supportive companion. He doesn't seek attention, nor does he require being in the spotlight. Podrick is "coachable" and eager to learn from those who are more knowledgeable than he is.

Possible disqualifying characteristics: His quiet nature often precludes him from being more assertive. Sometimes he "goes with the flow" when that isn't the best direction for his team.

Samwell Tarly

Description from the official GOT website: An overweight and timid, Night's Watch recruit who is forced to join after being disinherited by his family. He falls under Jon Snow's protection and becomes his best friend.

Qualifying characteristics: He is faithful and cares deeply for those in need. He demonstrates high levels of empathy, which compel him to take risks and break unjust rules in the service of his team.

Possible disqualifying characteristics: He has been known to cower in the face of danger. He's timid and generally avoids confrontation. (But then again, he did kill a White Walker!)

Do any of those descriptions sound like you? Do they remind you of someone on your team? How about the *possible disqualifying characteristics*? We all have shortcomings when it comes to being a good teammate. Some of us are naturally inclined to certain characteristics more so than others.

The ideal teammate would have Jon Snow's courage to take action, Breinne of Tarth's loyalty, Tyrion Lannister's willingness to invest in his role, Podrick Payne's humility and coachability, and Samwell Tarley's empathy.

We shouldn't be content to only be good at what comes naturally to us. We should strive to be great at every aspect of being a good teammate. Whether it's the *Game of Thrones* or the game of life, good teammates are committed to overcoming their flaws and building upon their natural abilities.

As always…Good teammates care. Good teammates share. Good teammates listen. Go be a good teammate.

For more Game of Thrones information, visit the shows official website: https://www.hbo.com/game-of-thrones

The Prince William Effect
MAY 21

Jumping to conclusions without trying to see an issue from another perspective is a poor method of operation. This is especially true in team settings.

Teammates create unnecessary drama when they rush to judgement before seeking alternative angles from which to view an issue. Being content to accept the most convenient point of view isn't just lazy, it's dangerous. Doing so causes needless division and leads to wasted time defending inaccuracies.

I like to refer to the drama spawned by teammates rushing to judgment as the *Prince William Effect*.

Shortly after the birth of their third child, the Duke and Duchess of Cambridge emerged from the hospital with their newborn. As the crowd greeted the Royal Couple, a photographer snapped a photo of Prince William appearing to stick his middle finger up at a reporter.

Outrage ensued as the photograph zoomed through social media. How could Prince William lower himself to such public crudeness?

As it turned out, he didn't. Another photographer captured the exact same moment from an alternative angle, and his photograph told a considerably different story.

Prince William was actually holding up three fingers, with his thumb holding down his index finger. He was joking to the reporter that he now had three children and "thrice the worry." His hand gesture only appeared to be a lone middle finger from the other angle.

Once the alternative photograph emerged, the controversy immediately ended. For Prince William, the controversy was rather benign as far as controversies go. But when similar scenarios play out on teams, the outcome is usually much more disruptive.

For example, let's say someone on your team is constantly arriving late. The simple explanation is this individual doesn't respect the team's time. Confronting the tardy teammate without seeing the issue from another perspective could cause him to be inappropriately branded, and his inevitable resentment could fracture the team.

Good teammates *peel back the layers of why?* before they accept the simple explanation.

Why is this teammate arriving late?
- Because he always oversleeps.

Why is he oversleeping?
- Because he goes to bed too late.

Why is he going to bed too late?
- Because he has a job that requires him to work a late shift.

Why is he working a job with a late shift?
- Because he needs extra money to cover his mother's medical bills.

What initially seemed like a careless, rude gesture—showing up late—turned out to be an understandable byproduct of an incredibly caring gesture—helping someone in need.

The only way for teams to avoid the potential destruction caused by the Prince William Effect is to *peel back the layers of why?* and seek alternative points of view. Good teammates care enough to realize they have a responsibility to view issues from other angles *before* they pass judgement.

As always…Good teammates care. Good teammates share. Good teammates listen. Go be a good teammate.

The Disillusioned Teammates
MAY 28

High school graduation season has arrived, and the signs of the "season" are unavoidable! Every store front has a prominent display of graduation cards and gifts, homes are adorned with yard signs boasting that a "Grad Lives Here," and social media is flooded with commencement photos and well-wishes.

Although the hoopla may arguably be a little cheesy, I still find the occasion inspiring. Graduation season is filled with hope and excitement for what the future holds. Families are proud of their graduates and graduates are proud of themselves. They finally made it.

But somewhere mixed in with all the smiles, commencement parties, and mortar board pix is a group of unfortunate souls—the forgotten graduates from last year. They were filled with the same optimistic spirit this time last year, only to return from their first year of college with a lot less zeal.

The next chapter of their lives hasn't played out to be quite as exciting as they had envisioned, and the optimistic graduates have become *the disillusioned graduates*. I saw a social media post this week from one of last year's graduates that reminded me just how *disillusioned* they can be. The post read:

All these high school seniors are like "can't wait to see what the next chapter holds." Gaining 15 pounds and spending $300 on a textbook, that's what it holds.

Wow! That is a shortsighted summation. I concede that for some the next chapter does include overpriced books and a decline in physical fitness. But that's not all it includes! The next chapter, especially for those attending college, also includes learning opportunities, finding resolve, and discovering talents you didn't even know you had.

Sometimes we encounter individuals on our team who are similar to the disillusioned graduates in that they too have become disenchanted. They're disappointed with their place on the team, and their disillusionment poses a potential threat to the team's culture.

When we encounter teammates like this, we need to remind them to stick with it and to keep grinding. They may not yet know what they don't know. Offering encouragement from your perspective of experience can be empowering to them. You understand that the current chapter, or even the next chapter, might include hardships. However, you also understand that those unpleasant experiences are part of the journey.

Reassure your disillusioned teammates that their current chapter isn't their last chapter, and their next chapter may be a set-up for their best chapter.

Sharing your knowledge and a little encouragement with disillusioned teammates struggling to grasp the need for patience and perseverance is a *good teammate move*. Go out of your way to convince them to stay the course.

And for those disillusioned graduates who happen to be reading this, realize that the "freshman 15" and $300 textbooks turn out to be minor, and eventually laughable, inconveniences. Don't let them deter you. Keep pushing on.

As always…Good teammates care. Good teammates share. Good teammates listen. Go be a good teammate.

By the way…

Looking for a Unique Graduation Gift? Many have used my children's book *Be a Good Teammate* as an alternative to a graduation card. It provides great life advice and has lots of space to write a personal message to your graduate! ("Be a Good Teammate" t-shirts make great graduation gifts too!) Visit *www.coachloya.com/store* to order.

Purposeful Acts of Kindness
JUNE 4

Last month, the governor of Pennsylvania officially declared May 23 as 1-4-3 Day in honor of native son Fred Rogers. The designation was intended to encourage the state's residents to "embrace the spirit of the kindest Pennsylvanian" by sharing acts of kindness with each other.

I grew up in Pennsylvania and loved *Mr. Roger's Neighborhood* as a kid. Watching the trolley travel to the Neighborhood of Make-Believe is among my favorite childhood memories. I was mesmerized by Daniel Tiger, King Friday, and Lady Fairchilde. And I remember a cardigan-wearing Mr. Rogers telling Mr. McFeely "1-4-3."

The number 143 held significance to Fred Rogers. It was code for "I love you," a message he frequently delivered to his neighborhood friends. The numbers represent the amount of letters in each of the words (I=1, Love=4, You=3). May 23 was chosen as the date to honor the children's television personality because it's the 143rd day of the year.

27

Mr. Rogers was kind. He embodied many of the qualities of a good teammate. Commemorating his legacy with a day dedicated to kindness is fitting.

Sometimes I come across schools and other organizations who try to improve their culture by encouraging *random acts of kindness*. They hold "R.A.K. Day" or "R.A.K. Week." I cringe whenever they use these terms. I understand what they're trying to accomplish, and I applaud their intentions. But I wish they would stop attaching the word "random" to their events because there should be nothing random about kindness.

Attaching the word random implies that the acts are done without reason. It suggests a lack of purpose and consistency. Mr. Rogers wasn't randomly kind; he was *consistently* kind. His kindness was filled with purpose, and yours should be to.

Good teammates choose kindness for a reason—to help their team. They're merciful, generous, and friendly towards their teammates in order to help their team achieve harmony, which leads to success. They don't help their team some of the time; they help their team *all* of the time.

Good teammates are not random. They are consistently purposeful.

If you're trying to encourage kindness at your school, in your organization, or on your team, eliminate the randomness that may be attached to your event. Instead of having a "R.A.K. Day," consider having a "P.A.K. Day" and celebrate *purposeful acts of kindness*.

That simple alteration will produce heightened levels of kindness and precisely the sort of shift in culture you desire.

Before you know it, your culture will be *packed* with kindness.

As always…Good teammates care. Good teammates share. Good teammates listen. Go be a good teammate.

Take Them Where They Are
JUNE 11

In my book *Building Good Teammates*, I wrote about a nun named Sister Eric Marie. I referred to her in the book as "That Nun," a nicknamed derived from how frequently people used to ask me about *that* nun hanging around the team I coached.

If you've read the book, you understand the designation became a term of endearment.

I am amazed by how often people ask me about Sister Eric Marie. When I speak at events, strangers who've read the book will come up to me and ask, "How's your nun doing?" or "Is your nun still alive?" Some even ask, "Is your nun a real person?"

I am humored by how *that* nun became *your* nun, like I have some type of exclusivity to her. I chuckle to myself whenever this happens, and then I assure the person asking that Sister Eric Marie is indeed a real person, she is still very much alive, and she is doing well.

Sister Eric Marie and I now live several states apart and have both transitioned to new missions since *Building Good Teammates* was published. But I talk to her regularly on the phone and through email, and I continue to marvel at her wisdom.

I recently posted a photo of Sister Eric Marie on social media, accompanied by the quote "Take them where they are." I directed the post to anyone working with students/players who come from difficult backgrounds.

Dealing with people who come from difficult backgrounds can be challenging work and can test your limits. These individuals can be filled with an odd mix of despair, ignorance, misguided beliefs, and overcompensation.

"Take them where they are" is Sister Eric Marie's philosophy of withholding judgment about other people's past. It's a way of focusing on the direction you want to help them go, while not being discouraged by *where* they presently are. It's resisting the urge to reject without attempting to understand. It's accepting the idea that we don't all start our journey in the same place.

Each of us is molded by the experiences of our lives, which have caused some of us to acquire social baggage and adopt a particular way of thinking. Unfortunately, that way of thinking doesn't always align with the team's culture.

In his book *Tattoos on the Heart*, Gregory Boyle writes about his work with Homeboy Industries and combating Los Angeles gangs. When unsavory-looking characters, covered in gang tattoos and wearing "standard-issue *barrio* apparel" come to him for help finding a job, he describes the need to see beyond their current appearance and present way of thinking.

He writes: "You need to dismantle shame and disgrace, coaxing out the truth in people who've grown comfortable believing its opposite." The truth is where people want to go is more significant than where they've been. This doesn't only apply to individuals with difficult backgrounds, it applies to all of us.

"Take them where they are" seems like leadership advice, but I think it's more like *good teammate* advice. You don't have to be the leader of your team to incorporate the philosophy into your mindset.

Good teammates are constantly nurturing the relationships they have with the other members on their team. To them, relationships are of paramount importance. Being too judgmental or unaccepting of someone else's past can prevent you from taking the relationship where you want it to go, which is why you must first care enough to accept others "where they are."

As always…Good teammates care. Good teammates share. Good teammates listen. Go be a good teammate.

A Frozen Mindset
JUNE 18

We often hear about the importance of people having a growth mindset—a belief that intelligence and ability can develop with time and experience. People who have this mentality value persistence and understand that extra effort can lead to higher levels of achievement.

The term "growth mindset" came from Stanford psychologist Carol Dweck and the discoveries she outlined in her bestselling book *Mindset*. According to Dweck's research, success can be heavily influenced by the way we view our talent and ability.

When we think of our talents as being malleable and capable of developing over time, we grow as individuals and tend to accept challenges with a positive outlook. The concept is occasionally simplified as embracing *The Power of Yet*, as in "I can't pass that test...*yet*." Or, "I can't do that move...*yet*." Or, "I don't know the answer...*yet*."

Good teammates have a growth mindset and it plays a significant role in how they influence their team. Having a growth mindset permits them to be purveyors of hope and sources of inspiration. It prevents them from bringing the team down by being derailed by failure.

But as important as it is for good teammates to have a growth mindset, it is equally important for them to also have a *Frozen mindset*.

To clarify, I'm not referring to a way of thinking that keeps them stuck in the same place. That's what Dweck describes as a "fixed mindset"—the exact opposite of a growth mindset. People with a fixed mindset believe their intelligence and ability are set at birth and cannot change. They avoid challenges and accept their limitations.

A fixed mindset hampers the team's progress, but a Frozen mindset moves the team forward. And by Frozen mindset, I mean a way of thinking that allows you to "let it go," as suggested by the theme song of the animated Disney film, *Frozen*.

When someone or something frustrates you, angers you, or offends you, sometimes the best course of action is to just *let it go* and move on. Obsessing over trivial issues can lead you to become unnecessarily distracted and stop you from focusing on what really matters.

You can become distracted to the point that your discontent is more toxic to your team than whomever or whatever wronged you. Having a Frozen mindset returns you to concentrating on team objectives and enables you to be a good teammate.

Anger can be motivating and can spur action. However, as a wise adage cautions, holding onto anger is like grasping a hot coal with the intent of throwing it at someone else; you are the one who gets burned.

Take a look at what angers you. Can you control it? Will addressing it make a significant difference to your team? If the answer is yes, then confront it. If the answer is no, then replace your misery with a melody, and *let it go*.

As always…Good teammates care. Good teammates share. Good teammates listen. Go be a good teammate.

9

Ten Ways to Express Gratitude
JUNE 25

Good teammates are grateful. They appreciate the people in their lives, are genuinely thankful when someone is kind to them, and never hesitate to express their gratitude.

Studies have consistently shown that individuals who are grateful experience better physical and mental health. They are also less likely to engage in toxic behaviors like jealousy and resentment, which is why having a proverbial "attitude of gratitude" can strengthen relationships between team members.

Here are ten ways for teammates to express gratitude:

1. Say "Thank you." It's the most obvious way and that's why we put it first on the list. However, a surprising amount of people underestimate the power of those two simple words—*thank you*. When spoken with sincerity, they can be the most motivating words in the English language.

2. Add an addendum. An addendum is a supplement that provides a little more information and a lot more potency. When you follow up "thank you" with an addendum phrase like "I appreciate this more than you'll ever know" or "You have no idea how much this means to me," you exponentially multiply the effects of your gratitude.

3. Touch them. A handshake, a pat on the back, or hug can also multiply the effectiveness of your words. Physical contact offers a transfer of energy, amplifying what we say. But make sure you're making physical contact at the right time. A good rule of thumb is touch when you are contributing to a person's self-esteem (compliments, praise, admiration, etc.), not when you're depleting (criticism, disapproval, discipline, etc.)

4. Give an unexpected gift. A small token of your appreciation (a cup of coffee, a piece of their favorite candy, a new pen, etc.) goes a long way. It doesn't have to be anything big, in fact small is probably better. I heard a story recently about a pop star who loved lip balm. One day a member of his staff bought him a tube of ChapStick, and the gift brought the pop star, who was known for being generous, to tears. Since the pop star already seemed to have everything that money could buy, people overlooked the impact a small gift like ChapStick could have on him.

5. Take them for a meal. Western civilizations celebrate their most important occasions with food (Christmas, Thanksgiving, wedding receptions, birthdays, anniversaries, etc.). Few things call for greater celebration than gratitude. Taking someone to lunch or buying that person dinner is a great way to show your appreciation because you gift them food and your time.

6. Acknowledge them publicly. Did someone help you? Did someone do something kind for you? Let others know about it! Become that person's biggest fan and publicly acknowledge him or her. Openly sing that person's praises to others.

7. Send a random text or email. Receiving an unexpected text or email letting you know you are appreciated makes your heart smile. You can read it over and over again. You can hold on to it and re-read it when you are down and need a *pick-me-up*. It's like plugging your heart into a battery charger.

8. Send a handwritten note. It may be old-fashioned, but it's still charming. A handwritten note carries the same value as a random text or email, only a handwritten note has the additional benefit of being able to be hung on a wall, so people other than just the recipient can experience your gratitude.

9. Like their posts. Liking and sharing someone's social media posts is a modern-day exercise in conveying emotion, especially gratitude. When you like, and even more so when you share, people's posts, you let them know you appreciate their willingness to allow you to witness their joy. Want to express more "social media" gratitude? Here's a secret: *love* their post, instead of just liking it. Did you know that Facebook, for instance, limits the number of friends who get to see a user's post? The more likes a post gets, the more people Facebook allows to see it. When you make the extra effort to click on the heart icon (love) instead of the thumbs up icon (like), you influence the Facebook algorithm and increase how many friends get to view a post. *Love* is always better than *like*.

10. Ask what you can do for them. We often assume saying thank you is enough, and in most cases it is. But don't be satisfied with that assumption. If people do something for you that is worthy of your gratitude, take the time to ask them if there is anything that you can do for them. Maybe there is, maybe there isn't. Even if declined, your offer to reciprocate reassures them that their actions moved you to being willing to act.

Expressing gratitude boosts happiness. Good teammates share their gratitude up, down, and across—meaning they thank those above them (their supervisors), those below them (their subordinates), and those across from them (their peers). Doing so extends their happiness in all directions.

It would be hypocritical of me to not take this opportunity to thank you for reading today's *Teammate Tuesday* entry. If you loved or shared this post on social media, then I am even more grateful *(You have no idea how much we appreciate it!)*.

And if there is anything our team can do to help you, please be sure to let us know.

As always…Good teammates care. Good teammates share. Good teammates listen. Go be a good teammate.

Clothier to General Washington
JULY 2

In a few days, America will celebrate it's 243rd birthday. This is the third time that our *Teammate Tuesday* blog has fallen during the week of Independence Day.

The first time, I wrote about the need for good teammates to become *independent* of the vices that hold them back. The second time, I wrote about General George Washington crossing the Delaware River and the need for good teammates to *cross the river* by mustering the courage to confront toxicity on their team.

Both of those are inspiring reads and I recommend you check them out if you haven't yet done so.

This Independence Day, I want to shine the spotlight on a key player in the American Revolution—Hercules Mulligan. Known as "Washington's Tailor," Hercules Mulligan operated a clothing emporium that catered to New York's upper echelon.

His position gained him acceptance among wealthy British businessmen and high-ranking soldiers. Mulligan would take their measurements and pass on secrets he overhead to the colonials. On at least two different occasions, he's credited with directly saving George Washington's life by predicting ambushes based on the dates British officers needed their mended uniforms returned.

Some call Hercules Mulligan a spy. Some label him a patriot. Others consider him a traitor. (A fair number of Brits follow this blog, so I want to make sure I am being sensitive to their perspective!)

I'd like to think that 243 years is enough time for everyone to discuss the American Revolution with objectivity. But just in case, I'm going to focus on two of Hercules Mulligan's traits that are shared by all good teammates and transcend the controversy of the aforementioned labels.

Number one: Hercules Mulligan was committed. He was "all in." Although he was born of European lineage, married to the daughter of a Royal Navy admiral, and lived among the British, his actions were dictated by his commitment to a cause in which he believed.

Was his belief in this this cause right or wrong? Doesn't matter. The point is he was committed to something he believed in. His actions weren't swayed by what he was supposed to be, nor by how others expected him to think. They were motivated by what he believed to be right and just. He was loyal to an ideal, not an entity.

Good teammates are committed to the standards of their team. Their loyalty to their team stems from their belief in what their team is attempting to accomplish—it's mission.

Number two: Hercules Mulligan was resilient. The British suspected him of collaborating with his Sons of Liberty cohorts on several occasions, for which he was occasionally beaten and imprisoned. But that didn't stop him. He remained committed.

In the Broadway musical *Hamilton*, Hercules Mulligan's character delivers a memorable line about his resiliency: "When you knock me down, I get the @#$% back up again!"

Although maybe a little on the crude side, that line sums up how good teammates handle adversity. They are not deterred by setbacks. When they get *knocked down*, they bounce back. They keep moving forward.

After the American Revolution ended, British loyalists were retaliated against. They were tarred and feathered and had their businesses burned to the ground. Hercules Mulligan feared retaliation for his perceived association with British officers—a credit to his ability to conceal his true loyalties.

A good teammate move by George Washington, however, quashed the possibility of retaliation against Mulligan. After an "Evacuation Day" celebration in New York, Washington visited Mulligan and shopped in his store. He continued to patronize Mulligan's store throughout his presidency, insisting that a sign be hung in front of the store identifying it as "Clothier to General Washington."

Happy Birthday, America! And thank you to Hercules Mulligan and all of the other good teammates who sacrificed for their beliefs.

As always…Good teammates care. Good teammates share. Good teammates listen. Go be a good teammate.

*Details about Hercules Mulligan are from "The Legend of Hercules Mulligan," Central Intelligence Agency, June 30, 2016, https://www.cia.gov/news-information/featured-story-archive/2016-featured-story-archive/the-legend-of-hercules-mulligan.html

11

Send 'Em Home with Anticipation
JULY 9

Contrary to a popular urban myth among students, teachers are not stored away in boxes over the summer break. Believe it or not, they actually continue to function as *normal* human beings.

Some of them have summer jobs. Some of them go on vacations with their families. Some of them even participate in professional development opportunities to become better teachers!

I recently spoke at a conference for educators about the art of being a good teammate. Sitting in the audience was a teacher who was preparing to enter her forty-third year in the classroom.

Kudos to her!

I try to engage the audience when I speak and get the attendees to share their experiences. Rarely do I leave an event without picking up a nugget or two of wisdom from my interactions with the audience. Their stories are insightful and often offer a perspective that I had not considered.

The teacher preparing for her forty-third year was especially insightful. You don't last that long in the teaching profession without loving your work and acquiring a sense of purpose.

She had a petite frame. Her hair was frosted by age and the lines on her face reflected her many years of working with wayward students. But she had a warm, welcoming smile that made people feel special.

Her smile was perfect for her line of work.

I asked the woman what she thought was the one thing she did best as a teacher. With a slight lisp and a hint of a southern drawl, she replied, "I send 'em home with anticipation."

The teacher went on to describe a sign on her desk that read: "Be someone who makes someone else look forward to tomorrow." She didn't know who said the quote, nor where she had even gotten the sign. But she did know that it was her constant source of inspiration. She was committed to being a *someone* who made others look forward to tomorrow.

When she sent her students home at the end of each school day, she made a point to tell them that she couldn't wait to see them back tomorrow. She sent them home with anticipation, eager to discover what the next day held.

Her students couldn't wait to return to school. They loved being with her and she let them know she loved being with them.

Good teammates embody this philosophy. They make the rest of the team look forward to tomorrow. Good teammates are pleasant to be around. They are energetic and their actions motivate us to act. We enjoy their company and they make us crave more.

How the veteran teacher sent her students home each day underscores the power of the words we choose. Sticks and stones may break bones, but words go straight to our hearts. Words can hurt or they can heal. Good teammates care enough to choose words that heal and provide hope. They use their words to make others look forward to tomorrow.

As always…Good teammates care. Good teammates share. Good teammates listen. Go be a good teammate.

12

State Your Empathy
JULY 16

Good teammates have an uncanny ability to empathize. They are hyperaware of their teammates' emotions and can slide into their teammates' shoes with the precision of a forensic psychologist.

Recognizing what it feels like to be in someone else's shoes is vital to healthy team dynamics. Empathy creates understanding, reduces conflict, and strengthens bonds. The more I analyze the art of being a good teammate, the more I realize how effective good teammates are at conveying their empathy.

Whenever I come to one of these realizations, I feel compelled to share what I have learned. This was the original purpose of the *Teammate Tuesday* blog.

Let's use the following hypothetical situation as an example: A teammate vents to you about something hurtful that another teammate said to him. You understand why he is upset, and you appreciate his frustration. However, you also understand that he took what was said out of context and is making too big of an issue of the situation.

Your advice is for your teammate to move on and *let it go*. Most would accept this to be a reasonable response, including good teammates. But before good teammates respond, they take one additional step: They state their empathy.

They articulate their assessment of the person's emotions before they dispense their advice. For instance, they might respond to the example above by saying, "You are upset. What was said hurt you, and I understand why you are frustrated. But my advice is for you to move on and let it go."

Even though those emotions may seem obvious, good teammates still state them.

Why? Because doing so reduces the probability of their response being taken the wrong way. Their response could be perceived as welcomed advice. It could also be perceived as insensitive criticism.

Good teammates don't want their response to add to the frustration. They want it to ease the tension.

A military axiom advises commanding officers to give orders that cannot be misinterpreted. Preceding a response by stating your empathy falls under the same heading. You make it clear to your teammates that you understand their emotional state.

By offering a brief recap, you validate their emotions and let them know you cared enough to put yourself in their shoes before passing judgment. Don't assume they realize you've done this. State your empathy and remove all doubt.

This simple gesture can have a huge impact on how well you're able to connect with your teammates. They will be far more likely to trust what you say to them when they know you understand how they are feeling.

If you are the type of person who struggles to empathize, try incorporating the technique of stating your empathy into your interactions. It will improve your ability to empathize and will make you a better teammate.

As always…Good teammates care. Good teammates share. Good teammates listen. Go be a good teammate.

In Lieu of Flowers
JULY 23

I am writing this edition of *Teammate Tuesday* with a heavy heart. After a prolonged battle with cancer, my sister passed away last week. Know that what follows is not a eulogy, but a lesson in living—a *good teammate* lesson.

Lana was the youngest of my five siblings. I was born at the other end of the spectrum, creating a significant age gap between us and leaving her forever engraved in my memory as a pigtailed little girl, holding the raggedy stuffed teddy bear she called "Muttley."

She of course grew up to be much more than that. After graduating college, my sister accepted a job as a teacher at a small, rural school. Her caring nature was a perfect match for the school's unique challenges, and she remained there for the duration of her career.

Had she moved on to a bigger school in a more affluent community, she could have avoided many of the difficulties that plagued her school—lower budgets, fewer extracurricular activities, lack of parental involvement, etc. But she never saw those issues as problems; she thought of them as opportunities to make a greater difference.

When the end of her life became imminent, my sister wrote her own obituary. At the end of it, she asked that donations of school supplies be sent to her beloved school in lieu of flowers. I found her request to exemplify the unusual generosity of a good teammate.

Instead of accepting rewards to which they are entitled, good teammates choose to redirect the resources used for the rewards to the needs of their teammates. Flowers are nice, but Lana knew she didn't need them. The students she loved, however, needed school supplies. She sacrificed her entitlement to benefit those for whom she cared. Her request is comparable to the MVP who deflects the credit to the other team members, or the child who wants money donated to his favorite charity instead of birthday presents, or the CEO who redistributes her quarterly bonus to her staff.

Those are all "good teammate moves" derived from love for something greater than themselves. We all have it within us to make those types of sacrifices.

If you're struggling to identify an *in lieu of flowers* sacrifice you can make, consider following Lana's example. Grab a backpack the next time you're at the store and fill it with school supplies to drop off at your local school. I assure you, your gesture will be appreciated and alter the course of a needy child's life.

As always…Good teammates care. Good teammates share. Good teammates listen. Go be a good teammate.

Like Mary's Dad
JULY 30

The world needs more people who think like Mary's dad. I suspect your immediate response is *Who's Mary's dad? And how does he think?* Let me elaborate.

My wife and I recently caught up with a friend whom we had not seen in a several years. This person had been a wonderful mentor to my wife. It was great talking with him and hearing everything that was going on in his life.

Our friend mentioned that his daughter, Mary, was doing especially well.

Mary had graduated college and was living in New York City. She was thriving in her new job, which she seemed to love, and growing her social circle. As if that weren't enough, an article she wrote had just been published in a prominent national magazine. Mary's life was headed in an exciting direction.

Her father commented that his ambition was to be known as "Mary's dad." What a wonderful perspective!

Good teammates think like Mary's dad. They aspire to be identified as their successful teammate's teammate. They aren't jealous or resentful of the label. In fact, being identified in this manner is a tremendous source of happiness for them because they want their actions to propel the success of those around them.

When you invest in the members of your team you cannot help but feel a connection to their success.

Mary's dad has achieved plenty in his own right and has much to be proud of. But individual success isn't what drives him. He wants to help the other members of his team (family) achieve. He wants his daughter's success to reach a point where it overshadows his. He *wants* to be known as "Mary's dad."

Teams can be consumed by toxicity when members become jealous of each other's individual success. Egos grow fragile and referring to someone as *so and so's* teammate can be a divisive insult.

Mary's dad was comfortable enough to share an *egoless* relationship with his daughter. He sacrificed to provide her with opportunities. He encouraged her to pursue greatness and conveyed his belief in her ability to do so. He empowered her with confidence. But he respected the fact that she was the one who ultimately made it happen.

Mary's dad didn't try to put an asterisk beside his daughter's success. He didn't claim credit for it, and he didn't try to live vicariously through her. He simply took pride in his contributions.

In other words, he didn't live through her, he lived for her. His intention was for his contributions to lead to his daughter's success.

Do you care enough about your teammates to help them succeed? Are you comfortable enough with your own contributions to aspire to be known as your teammate's teammate? If you are truly a good teammate, then the answer is yes.

As always...Good teammates care. Good teammates share. Good teammates listen. Go be a good teammate.

Just Share Your Love
AUGUST 6

Becky called Herb with some exciting news. She had just been hired as a teacher at her alma mater. It would be her first full-time teaching job since graduating college. However, her hiring came with one small caveat; she was required to also coach the school's soccer team.

Herb had been Becky' soccer coach in college and an influential presence in her life. While Becky was excited to finally secure a full-time teaching position, she was nervous about the prospect of coaching. She was calling Herb to get coaching advice.

Herb thought about what he should say to her. Becky had been a joy to coach. She bought into the team's culture and got along well with her fellow teammates. She worked hard and pushed herself further than her abilities should have allowed. The driving force behind Becky's play had always been her love for the game.

But like a lot of players, Becky had never put much thought into the nuances of coaching. She had only ever viewed the game through a player's eyes. Herb suspected Becky realized this and her realization was the source of her anxiety.

The responsibility to order equipment, devise game plans, manage personalities, and organize practice sessions seemed overwhelming to her.

Herb also knew that Becky lacked the experience to appreciate the influence she would soon have on her players' lives. She didn't understand that the octogenarians that gather in the mornings at the local coffee shop may forget the names of their grandchildren, but they can recall with vivid clarity the hurtful and/or inspiring words their coach spoke to them in their youth. A coach's words are like tattoos on a player's soul.

Herb didn't want to compound Becky's anxiety by calling attention to this reality, so he boiled his advice down to one simple sentence. He told her to "just share your love for the game with your players."

He knew if she stuck to that single charge, everything would fall into place. She would find the energy to seek the best game plans and incorporate the right drills. She would be organized and prepared. She would reveal details about her experiences as a player. And above all, she would never deliberately say or do anything that would taint her players' potential love of the game.

Herb's advice captures the *modus operandi* of good teammates. They show they care by sharing their love for their team. His advice applies to new coaches, new teachers, new bosses, and anyone who wants to make a difference on their team.

When you share your love, caring eventually shines through all aspects of your craft—whatever craft that happens to be.

I was back-to-school shopping with my daughters last week and saw a t-shirt with the message "Radiate Kindness" printed on it. I saw several shirts broadcasting similar messages at different stores we visited, and I love the idea that promoting kindness has become fashionable.

Good teammates radiate kindness…and enthusiasm…and *love for their team.* They radiate them through every pore of their bodies, during every second of their days. Their willingness to do this is what differentiates them from average teammates.

As always…Good teammates care. Good teammates share. Good teammates listen. Go be a good teammate.

Unconquerable Gladness
AUGUST 13

Franklin D. Roosevelt had a sign on his desk that read: "Let unconquerable gladness dwell." The sign was a source of encouragement for America's thirty-second president.

I've been thinking a lot about that sign's meaning. The more I ponder the words, the more I realize how accurately they describe the challenge of being a good teammate. So many of the choices good teammates are compelled to make are counter to what comes easily.

It's easy to choose what is best for you instead of choosing what is best for your team. It's easy to complain about problems instead of confronting problems. It's easy to jump ship instead of weathering the storm.

But the *easy* way isn't necessarily the good teammate way.

Having to constantly choose the more difficult route can be exhausting. The toll of "doing the right thing" can wear you down. And therein lies the challenge of being a good teammate: To not allow difficult choices to break your spirit.

Good teammates cannot permit their spirit to be conquered by collateral negativity. Part of being glad is being joyful. However, gladness is additionally about being willing. Good teammates are both joyful and willing. They eagerly serve the needs of their team and derive happiness from doing so.

When you thank a good teammate, the response is inevitably along the lines of "I am *glad* to help." Good teammates are filled with gladness. They don't see difficult choices as challenges; they see them as opportunities, for which they are grateful.

Franklin D. Roosevelt served his country during a difficult period in its history. He was challenged by a Great Depression, a Great World War, and a not-so-great personal battle with polio. It doesn't take much to see the need for the sign that sat on his desk.

The origin of Roosevelt's sign came from a prayer book distributed to soldiers in WWII. The actual passage in the book included several preceding words: "At the heart of all our trouble and sorrow let unconquerable gladness dwell."

At the heart of a good teammate dwells a commitment to caring about the team. Choosing to be a good teammate can make you vulnerable to trouble and sorrow. It's true. But the choice can also lead you to experience incredible happiness. When you care enough to let your choices be dictated by a cause greater than yourself—the needs of your team—you allow unconquerable joy to dwell in *your* heart.

As always…Good teammates care. Good teammates share. Good teammates listen. Go be a good teammate.

17

What's Best for My Team?
AUGUST 20

Oakland Raiders wide receiver Antonio Brown has been in the headlines lately over a dispute about his helmet. The helmet Brown has worn for the duration of his career is no longer approved for use in the National Football League, and the all-pro player is resisting the mandate to transition to the new design.

I don't know Antonio Brown, and I have no direct knowledge of his situation. I am reluctant to allow my opinions to be swayed by third hand accounts or cleverly spliced news clips that may portray biased narratives. For those reasons, I am not advocating for or against Antonio Brown's stance.

Furthermore, I try to keep *Teammate Tuesdays* free of negativity or controversial topics. My objective is to help readers understand and cultivate the mindset of a good teammate. I only mention Antonio Brown's name to provide context to a quote I read over the weekend from a retired professional football player that I feel offers insight into a good teammate's mentality.

When asked about Antonio Brown's situation, former Seattle Seahawks wide receiver Doug Baldwin explained to USA Today why players wouldn't want to switch to a newer, safer helmet.

"Their argument is it comes back to aesthetics: This (old) helmet is sleeker, it looks better, whatever the case may be. That's just—to me personally, as a husband and as a father— it's just not a sound argument," Baldwin said.

Baldwin also wore the same helmet for most of his career, but he switched to one of the newer, safer helmets once he realized how much more likely they were to protect his head from injury. He loved his old helmet. It was lighter, smaller, and more comfortable to him. The data, however, was too compelling for him to overlook.

Baldwin's rationale for switching helmets illustrates the decision-making process of a good teammate. He considered the risks of continuing to use his old helmet and what sustaining a head injury would mean to his immediate team (his wife and children). When he factored their long-term wellbeing into the equation, his decision became an easy choice.

Most people tend to only consider what is best for themselves. They don't think about how their decisions affect the other members of their team. They think *What is best for me?* instead of *What is best for my team?*

Unfortunately, that is the sort of selfish thinking that causes toxicity on teams—and not just sport teams, either. All teams (communities, families, staffs, etc.) breakdown when the basis for decisions becomes self-serving, as opposed to team-serving.

Good teammates see beyond the instant gratification of their decisions. They're aware of the ripple effect of their actions and are mindful of the big picture. Because of that, they're willing to sacrifice their comfort zone for the betterment of their team. They are able to endure inconveniences for the sake of their teammates.

You may not be involved in a "helmet" problem on your team, but you might be entangled in a selfishness problem. If so, consider whether you are thinking *What's best for me?* Or *What's best for my team?* Your solution will be found in your answer.

As always…Good teammates care. Good teammates share. Good teammates listen. Go be a good teammate.

*The interview with Doug Baldwin referenced above is from Tom Schad, "For former NFL player Doug Baldwin, embracing newer helmet technology was a no-brainer," USA Today, August 18, 2019, https://www.usatoday.com/story/sports/nfl/2019/08/18/doug-baldwin-no-reason-nfl-players-not-wear-safer-helmets/2032555001/

18

Because We've Seen a Thing or Two
AUGUST 27

I find the Farmers Insurance "Hall of Claims" commercials to be especially well done. They're clever and humorous.

If you're unfamiliar with the commercials, they show actor J.K. Simmons walking prospective clients through the fictitious Farmers Insurance Hall of Claims—a large room filled with monuments paying tribute to the company's "most unbelievable but true claims."

The monuments include such bizarreness as the *Trucksicle* (a pickup truck that fell through the ice when an overly confident fisherman drove onto an insufficiently frozen lake) and the *Billy Goat Ruffians* (a goat who repeatedly rammed his head into the door of a shiny SUV, unaware that he was headbutting his own reflection.)

The commercials always end with J.K. Simmons delivering Farmers' trademark tagline: "At Farmers, we know a thing or two because we've seen a thing or two."

Their tagline implies that customers can rely on Farmers Insurance because they've got experience. As consumers, we value experience. We want our ailments to be treated by experienced doctors. We want our cars to be repaired by experienced mechanics. We want our finances to be managed by experienced accountants.

We want experience because experience equates to trust—an important component of meaningful relationships. We need to *trust* that the other half of the relationship knows what they are doing. The more they've seen and done, the less likely they are to make a mistake; and the more likely we are to trust them.

Experience comes with time. The longer we do something the more experienced we become. But an underlying assumption accompanies the trust we place in experience: We trust that mistakes won't be repeated.

Repeated mistakes become bad habits and relying on people with bad habits is ill-advised. Good teammates understand the difference between making mistakes and making *repeated* mistakes.

Mistakes happen, especially when we are growing and trying to expand the parameters of our comfort zones. Mistakes are part of the process. But the experience gained from dealing with those mistakes should equip us to prevent them from happening again. In other words, we should learn from our mistakes and vow not to repeat them.

You don't have to be experienced to be a good teammate. But you do need to convey to the other members of your team a commitment to not repeat your mistakes or the mistakes of anyone else on your team. That type of commitment requires heightened awareness and tremendous self-discipline—two benchmarks of a person who cares.

Good teammates know a thing or two because they care about more than just a thing two. Feel free to let the Farmers Insurance jingle play in your head now. *We are Good Teammates! Bum ba dum bum bum bum bum.*

As always…Good teammates care. Good teammates share. Good teammates listen. Go be a good teammate.

Using Shame to Motivate

SEPTEMBER 3

If you use social media with any sort of regularity, you've surely come across an *I'll bet I won't even get one like* post. The post is accompanied by an image intended to tug at your heart strings and compel you to click the "like" button. They usually feature a photo of a World War II veteran celebrating his 100ᵗʰ birthday, or a hairless cancer patient undergoing chemo, or an abused dog covered in scars.

I realize the expression *tug at your heartstrings* is a cliché, but this is exactly what these images do. They reach out and grab the deepest part of our souls and pull our emotions out of us. Who isn't moved by these images?

The problem with the *I'll bet I won't even get one like* posts is the tactic used to illicit action. They try to guilt us into acting. They manipulate our emotions by making us feel shame if we don't click the "like" button.

Manipulation and shame are not tactics good teammates use to illicit action. Good teammates don't blame, shame, or complain. They inspire.

If you have to manipulate your teammates' emotions by guilting them to act you will never get their best. Their actions will only be fueled by obligation, and never by commitment. If you're lucky, your teammates will meet the minimal expectation. But they will never reach a point where they are inspired to champion a cause.

In *Building Good Teammates: The Story of My Mount Rushmore, a Coaching Epiphany, and That Nun*, I recounted the story of the advice Warren Buffett gave to U2 frontman Bono for how to get Americans to join the battle to end poverty in Africa.

Buffett told Bono: "Don't appeal to the conscience of America. Appeal to the greatness of America." In other words, Bono would fail if he were to guilt Americans into helping with his cause. *How can the citizens of the wealthiest nation in the world stand by idly and not care about this problem?* Instead, Bono needed to inspire Americans. *You're the greatest country in the world, if anybody can help solve this problem, it is you.*

Guilting teammates into service is compliance. Inspiring teammates to serve is commitment. Commitment always produces better results than compliance. Good teammates are rooted in commitment.

By the way, those *I'll bet I won't get one like* posts are manipulative in more than one way. Cyber-security experts have discovered them to be a form of "like-farming." Scammers prey on users' emotions to "like" their post. Since social media algorithms reward popularity, the more "likes" a post gets, the higher the probability of it appearing on someone else's timeline.

When the post gains sufficient popularity, the scammers go back and replace the original content with malware or some other type of harmful content. If you've ever shared one of those posts, go back and look at your history. You may discover you inadvertently liked a page or shared something you didn't intend.

As always...Good teammates care. Good teammates share. Good teammates listen. Go be a good teammate.

The Gallbladder Lesson
SEPTEMBER 10

I put the finishing touches on this week's edition of *Teammate Tuesday* from the confines of my hospital bed while I waited to be wheeled away for gallbladder surgery.

A few months ago, I experienced the first of what my doctors later determined to be gallbladder attacks. The attacks began with a sharp pain in my back that gradually spread to the upper right side of my abdomen. The pain was accompanied by a spike in my temperature and intense nausea.

After enduring several subsequent attacks, with the most recent resulting in a trip to the emergency room, doctors decided that the best course of action was to remove my gallbladder.

I've been thinking about how my gallbladder problem mirrors the issue of handling a toxic teammate.

The gallbladder is basically a hollow organ that stores excess bile, a sort of digestive lubricant. Most of the time the gallbladder lies dormant like a deflated balloon. But between meals, it fills with bile and temporarily grows to the size of a small pear. The gallbladder has a purpose, but it's not an essential organ. The human body can adapt and function perfectly fine without it.

However, when the gallbladder malfunctions the human body is thrust into turmoil. If not dealt with, toxins literally spew into the rest of the body. I can attest from personal experience that a malfunctioning gallbladder equates to complete misery. How can something so small and nonessential create such a disruption in harmony?

The misery caused by a malfunctioning gallbladder is a lot like the misery caused by a malfunctioning teammate—even a *nonessential* teammate.

Occasionally, teams have individuals who become, for whatever reason, disgruntled. Maybe they don't like their role. Maybe they feel underappreciated. Or maybe they've become unable to operate within the boundaries of a team-first culture. As their malcontent grows, so does the probability of them disrupting the team's functionality.

The disruptions they cause aren't always proportional to the individual's prominence on the team. Disgruntled benchwarmers can be just as disruptive as star players. Malcontent receptionists can be just as disruptive as top sales representatives.

When my gallbladder first started to malfunction, we tried to manage the situation with medication and diet. We made an honest effort to correct the malfunction without taking extreme measures. Ultimately, our efforts failed and surgery became our most viable solution.

When a teammate is malfunctioning, you need to follow a similar strategy. Do your due diligence and make him or her aware of *your* perception of the toxic behavior. Explain why the behavior is unacceptable. Be clear about the alterations you expect. Provide the support and encouragement needed to make the necessary alterations. But understand that those steps might not resolve the problem.

Comparable to my gallbladder situation, sometimes removing the malfunctioning teammate from the team is the best course of action.

This is not a decision that good teammates arrive at lightly. Take solace in knowing that if you've exhausted your other options removing a toxic teammate is your way of prioritizing the interests of your team. Your decision is your way of showing how much you *care* about your team.

As always...Good teammates care. Good teammates share. Good teammates listen. Go be a good teammate.

Nonessential Teammates
SEPTEMBER 17

Last week, I wrote about my gallbladder surgery. I am delighted to report that the operation was a success and that I am steadily headed down the road to recovery. The amount of well-wishes I received was humbling, and I would like to take this opportunity to thank everyone who reached out to me.

The message from last week's blog is best summarized as: Toxic teammates are like malfunctioning gallbladders in that sometimes the only viable remedy is to remove them (from the team).

I mentioned, as a side note, that disruptions aren't always proportional to an individual's prominence on the team. Disgruntled benchwarmers can be just as disruptive as star players. I tried to use the analogy of my gallbladder to explain the extent of the misery that can be caused by such a small and seemingly insignificant organ. In mentioning this, I inadvertently muddied my main point about removing malfunctioning teammates by using the term *nonessential* to describe teammates with less prominent roles.

Mixed in with the many well-wishes I received were a pair of emails from readers who questioned my use of the *nonessential* label. Their objections were worthy and necessitate clarification.

I believe everybody on the team is essential. A leader's job is to assemble a team comprised of the minimum number of teammates needed to achieve the maximum efficiency. If you're on the team, then it should be assumed that your role *is* essential; ergo, you are an essential teammate.

I was attempting to point out that *any* malfunctioning member can derail a team. Think of the many talented chefs who've had their restaurants fail because of poor service. Chefs spend their entire lives honing their culinary skills and acquiring savory recipes, only to have inattentive wait staffs sully their restaurants' reputations. Yelp is filled with one-star reviews citing good food, but lousy service.

Comparable scenarios are true for doctors' offices, car dealerships, and almost any other business. Everybody on the team is essential.

However, I also believe that nobody on the team is essential. I had hoped my italicizing the word *nonessential* in last week's post would convey the duality of my thoughts. That obviously didn't happen.

Everybody is essential if we interpret essential to mean valuable. Nobody is essential if we define essential as irreplaceable. Both statements are accurate.

The most talented chef in the world will fail if he is disruptive to his restaurant. His culinary skills won't matter, nor will his sought-after recipes. His toxic disposition will prevent his restaurant from reaching its potential.

Again, the same is true for talented doctors, car salesmen, and athletes who are toxic teammates. Their toxicity will eventually overtake their talents and their teams will fail. Keeping them on the team and tolerating their toxicity will always be hazardous.

Good teammates understand the significance of every team member, as well as the replaceability of every team member. They have the confidence to accept that nobody is ever better than them, and the humility to appreciate that nobody is ever beneath them.

The *duality* of that perspective is what makes good teammates essential to any team's success.

As always…Good teammates care. Good teammates share. Good teammates listen. Go be a good teammate.

Five Ways Good Teammates Unintentionally Fail
SEPTEMBER 24

Being a good teammate isn't always easy. You try your best to put the needs of the team before your own, but sometimes your efforts to do that end up causing more harm than good. Here are five ways you can unintentionally fail in your attempt to be a good teammate:

1. Enable: Helping your teammate is great until your help becomes counterproductive. When you start doing tasks for your teammate that he could and should be doing for himself, you do your teammate a disservice. You become an enabler. While your willingness to help is commendable, be sure you aren't facilitating your teammate's self-destructive behavior or encouraging his ineptitude. Enablers unintentionally foster team toxicity.

2. Oblige: Similar to the enabler, an obliger's desire to help is commendable. But if you become too accommodating, trying to oblige every request, you risk burning yourself out. A burnt-out teammate cannot effectively serve the needs of the team—ergo, a burnt-out teammate cannot be a good teammate. You must be able to prioritize your teams and decline opportunities that jeopardize your mental or physical wellbeing.

3. Lack Awareness: Do any of your teammates have annoying habits? Well, you probably do too! Good teammates tend to have a high tolerance for their teammates' annoying idiosyncrasies like talking loud, chewing with their mouth open, or biting their fingernails. But just because you are tolerant of others' idiosyncrasies doesn't mean they will respond the same way towards yours. Good teammates don't make this assumption. Good teammates are mindful of their annoying habits and make a deliberate effort to avoid engaging in them. Incidentally, being too tolerant of your teammates' annoying idiosyncrasies cultivates dysfunction and turns you into an enabler.

4. Be Stubborn: Not every issue is worth digging your heels in and preparing for battle. Good teammates know the difference between a preference and a necessity. For example, let's say your teammate wants to work out before going home. But you want to go home, get something to eat, and workout later. Your way makes more sense. You've had a long day and you're already tired. Why not wait until later when you are fresh and can give a more concentrated effort? Working out later is a preference, not a necessity. Your teammate wanting to work out before going home is also a preference and not a necessity. The issue doesn't have any deadlines or severe consequences, only a preferred methodology. Good teammates understand the difference between a preference and a necessity. They save their energy for battles over necessities. When it comes to disagreements over preferences, a good policy to abide by is to go with the method of the person to whom it matters more. If doing something a particular way is more important to the other person, then adopt a "Frozen Mindset" (*see Chapter 8) and do it their way. Don't let your stubbornness turn you into a *teambuster*.

5. Complain Instead of Confront: You've got a problem on your team that you want to remedy. The problem is legitimate and so is your desire to resolve it. You decide to raise awareness and talk about the problem to anybody who will listen. The wheel that squeaks the loudest gets the oil, right? Wrong. The issue is that not everybody who's willing to listen can do something about your problem. By talking about the problem with unfocused precision, you've transformed yourself into a complainer. Complaining could cause you to be a greater source of toxicity than the problem you were originally complaining about. You don't want to complain about the problem, you want to confront the problem. Confronting means addressing the problem directly to the source or to someone who is in a position to influence the source, like a supervisor. Remember: The wheel that squeaks the loudest doesn't always get the oil. Sometimes it simply gets replaced.

As always…Good teammates care. Good teammates share. Good teammates listen. Go be a good teammate.

Fiberglass Teammates
OCTOBER 1

If you Google the word clique, you'll find the top search
result to be the Oxford Dictionary definition: *a small group of
people, with shared interests or other features in common, who
spend time together and do not readily allow others to join them.*

That definition sounds a lot like the definition of a team.
But cliques are nothing like teams. Cliques are mini-groups
within the team that destroy the team from the inside out.
Cliques prevent teams from reaching their potential. Cliques
are bad.

However, just because cliques are bad doesn't mean
everyone in the clique is bad. Assuming that cliques always
form out of dissention would be a mistake. Sure, some cliques
are the clustering of malcontents dissatisfied with team policy.
But most cliques are the result of individuals hesitant to
venture outside of their comfort zones.

In sports, they're seniors who only hang out with other
seniors. They're defensive players who only hang out with

other defensive players. In the workplace, they're salesmen who only fraternize with other salesmen. They're marketing associates who only partner with other associates in their department.

The best teams are comprised of fiberglass teammates.

Fiberglass is a versatile product, used to make auto parts, boats, airplanes, surfboards, and bathtubs. In fact, Owens Corning cites over 40,000 fiberglass applications. The appeal being that fiberglass is stronger, lighter, cheaper, and more flexible that many metals.

Fiberglass is literally made from glass—the same glass used to make windows, wine bottles, chandeliers, etc. Fiberglass is produced by forcing molten glass through microfine strainers that produce thin "threads" of glass. Those threads are then randomly woven together and mixed with resin.

What's interesting about fiberglass is that it isn't the resin that gives the product its strength—it's the number of connections made between the tiny brittle glass threads. The more fibers touching each other, the stronger the fiberglass.

The situation for successful teams is similar. Fiberglass teammates make a deliberate effort to connect with as many of their fellow teammates as they can. Every connection they make bonds them to another teammate. Bonded teammates are connected teammates. Connected teammates are fiberglass teammates. Fiberglass teammates thwart cliques.

Becoming a fiberglass teammate may require you to get out of your comfort zone and interact with members of your team who you normally would not. This may entail you having to mix up your usual routine. Maybe you'll need to eat lunch with a different group of teammates or even take your lunch break at a different time.

But sacrificing the convenience of your comfort zone to connect with more teammates will strengthen your team and lead you to become a good teammate.

As always...Good teammates care. Good teammates share. Good teammates listen. Go be a good teammate.

*Statistics about Owens Corning's applications are from Mitch Jacoby, "What's Fiberglass, and How Does the Delicate Material Reinforce Thousands of Products," Chemical & Engineering News, Volume 96, Issue 38, September 22, 2018, https://cen.acs.org/materials/inorganic-chemistry/s-fiberglass-does-delicate-material/96/i38

When Prudence Drives
OCTOBER 8

I have heard it said that humility is the basis for all other virtues because humility is how we see ourselves. Good teammates practice humility. They see themselves as subordinate to their team.

Good teammates commit to being governed by the premise that they will never be bigger than their team. No matter how much individual success they achieve, good teammates refuse to view themselves as being more important than the team. Their understanding and acceptance of this premise defines them.

Humility is what allows the head coach to grab a broom and sweep the gym floor. Humility is what permits the company's CEO to refill the copier. Humility is what allows us to assess our talents and be receptive to using them to help our team.

Of the many good teammate virtues that stem from humility, prudence may be my favorite.

Prudence is not a common word, nor is it a word most people use to describe good teammates. But maybe it should be. Prudence is the ability to discipline oneself through one's knowledge. In layman's terms, prudence is making sound decisions based on what you know to be true.

We often see the word prudence associated with frugality or conservative business practice. In sports, prudence is sometimes used to explain conservative coaching decisions, like football coaches who opt to punt the ball instead of going for it on fourth and short.

Because prudence is at times associated with *playing it safe*, the term receives an undeserved stigma. Prudence isn't limited to conservatism. Prudence is being knowledgeable *and* being willing to act on that knowledge.

Good teammates can be conservative, but they can also be risk takers. The aspect of prudence that applies to good teammates is that their judgment is based on knowledge. In this instance, that knowledge being that they, as individuals, are never more important than their team.

When good teammates take risks, they weigh the consequences. They consider the possible benefit or damage that their decision will have on their team and they act accordingly. They don't consider the possible benefit or damage their decision will have on them as an individual.

Good teammates don't seek individual glory; they seek team success.

Why? Because they practice humility. They believe that their individual accolades are the byproducts of their commitment to serving the needs of their team.

Arrogance is the result of seeing yourself as greater than you are. Arrogant teammates can never be good teammates because their motives will never fully align with the team's agenda. If you want to ward off arrogance, start exercising prudence.

When prudence drives your decisions, team success will inevitably follow.

As always…Good teammates care. Good teammates share. Good teammates listen. Go be a good teammate.

Managing Inconvenience
OCTOBER 15

The past few months have proven to be a bit of a tough stretch for my family. I lost my sister to cancer in July and my father passed away last week. At my father's funeral, someone remarked that "tough times create tough people."

That may be true, but what I've found to be more applicable is that tough times reveal good teammates.

Tracey Lawrence had a country song out a few years ago titled "Find Out Who Your Friends Are." The song was about the lengths to which true friends will go during our time of need. The chorus was as follows:

You find out who your friends are
Somebody's gonna drop everything
Run out and crank up their car
Hit the gas get there fast
Never stop to think 'what's in it for me?'
or 'it's way too far.'

They just show on up with their big old heart
You find out who you're friends are

I grow emotional when I think of how much support I've received over the past few months. The many phone calls, texts, and emails have been comforting. I've had friends who were exhausted from working all day drive hours to show their support. I've had friends use vacation days just to "be there" for me.

My friend Scott took me to lunch on Saturday, so we could talk one-on-one and I could get a break from the stress. Scott has a demanding job. He works long hours and his weekends are needed for family time and to catch up with chores around his house. Taking time out of his schedule to eat lunch with me was not convenient for him.

But Scott and all the others never thought *what's in it for me?* or *it's way too far*, and they never concerned themselves with being inconvenienced.

We call them friends, but they are teammates—*good* teammates. And they represent the difference between how the three types of teammates manage inconvenience.

Bad teammates (who I like to refer to as *teambusters*) never mind inconveniencing others, yet they hate to be inconvenienced by others.

Neutral teammates try not to inconvenience others, but they also hate to be inconvenienced.

Good teammates go out of their way—sometimes enduring tremendous personal sacrifice—in order to not inconvenience others. Yet they never seem to mind being inconvenienced by anyone or anything that benefits their team.

As the Tracey Lawrence song suggests, good teammates are the ones who show up when you *run your car off the side of the road and get stuck in a ditch way in the middle of nowhere.* If you have these types of teammates on your team, be grateful. If you are this type of teammate, be proud. You make the world a better place.

As always…Good teammates care. Good teammates share. Good teammates listen. Go be a good teammate.

26

Rain Dancers
OCTOBER 22

The rain dance is traditionally associated with Native American tribes from the southwestern United States. But the rain dance is far from exclusive to Native Americans.

For generations, dances intended to invoke rain were a regular part of tribal life in parts of Africa, China, and Thailand. Rain dances have even been documented in some Eastern European cultures. In all these regions, rain was essential to agriculture and, ultimately, survival. Without rain, life was unbearable.

Did the dances actually influence the weather? Probably not. Did the dances influence the psyche of the tribe? Most definitely.

The one constant among those who engaged in the ritual was that the dances were always led by the groups' most influential figures—the chiefs, the shamans, and the kings. These individuals got the rest of the tribe to participate and believe in the dance's purpose.

What sometimes gets lost in the mystique of the rain dance is that the rituals were highly choreographed. The dance steps were intricate and left little room for improvisation. Comparatively, the dances that occurred once the rain started to fall were much more spontaneous. Those dances were raw and celebratory. People were genuinely thankful and happy to be dancing in the rain.

A favorite quote of mine, often attributed to artist/author Vivian Green, is: "Life isn't about waiting for the storm to pass. It's about learning how to dance in the rain."

Working with others can be emotionally taxing, especially during difficult times. If you allow yourself to be fooled into thinking you'll be happy and able to get along with everybody once the difficulty passes, you'll soon discover yourself to be entangled in stress.

Being part of a competitive team is stressful by nature. Your involvement is a constant matter of give-and-take, sacrifice, and prioritizing team needs over individual wants—all of which can be exacerbated by the team's struggle to succeed.

Good teammates are gifted with the willingness to remain loyal and weather their teams' metaphorical storms. Their stick-to-it-ness can hold their teams together during difficult times. But more importantly, good teammates can also dance in the rain.

Good teammates are *rain dancers*, not in that their intentions are to conjure precipitation, but in that they are able to value the journey and find happiness despite the journey's challenges.

Because our emotions impact those around us, the ability to dance in the rain is an essential skill for anyone who is part of a team. Much like the chiefs, shamans, and kings who influenced their tribes, good teammates influence the emotional well-being of their fellow team members by dancing in the rain.

The chiefs, shamans, and kings weren't concerned about how they looked or what others thought of their dancing. Their concern was helping their teams. The same is true for good teammates.

As always…Good teammates care. Good teammates share. Good teammates listen. Go be a good teammate. teammate.

Details about Native American tribal dancing are from "Rain Dance: The History and Ritual of the Rain Dance Is Still Followed Today," Indians.org, http://indians.org/articles/rain-dance.html

Sharpen the Chisel
OCTOBER 29

Are you familiar with the parable about the woodcutter and his dulling axe? Several variations of the parable float around the Internet, but the basic premise is as follows:

A man is hired to chop down trees. Filled with zeal and intent on impressing his new boss, the man heads into the woods with his axe. He returns at the end of his first day having chopped down an inordinate number of trees.

The second day, however, he cuts down fewer trees. He tries harder the third day but cuts down even fewer trees than the previous day. After continuing to cut down fewer and fewer trees, the man apologizes to his boss, confessing that he doesn't understand why he isn't being more productive despite trying harder.

His boss responds by asking him when he last sharpened his axe, to which the man replies that he's been so busy cutting down trees that he hasn't had time to sharpen his axe.

The woodcutter story reminds me of an often-cited Abraham Lincoln quote: "If I had five minutes to chop down a tree, I'd spend the first three sharpening my axe."

Like the woodcutter story, several variations of Lincoln's quote also float around the Internet. But they all share the same meaning. Both Lincoln's quote and the woodcutter story and are meant to emphasize the importance of paying attention to those elements that make us most effective—something good teammates commit to doing.

While I get the woodcutter story and like its message, I think the moral is delivered through a flawed example. I don't mind the dull axe, but I dislike the idea of chopping wood.

Who enjoys chopping wood? Nobody. Chopping wood is a chore. Chopping wood is not fun. I grew up in a rural area and chopped plenty of wood as a kid. I can attest from personal experience that chopping wood—though necessary—is a hard, unpleasant task.

I think a better analogy is a sculptor needing to sharpen his chisel. The same parameters apply, except that it is easier to see purpose in the sculptor's work. The sculptor isn't engaging in an unpleasant task like chopping wood, he's chipping away at the stone keeping him from creating his masterpiece.

Creating a masterpiece is a labor of love. With the approaching release of my new book, *The WE Gear*, a lot of my time lately has been spent in meetings and on conference calls discussing marketing strategies, early projections, and sales algorithms—none of which particularly interest me.

I don't want to be occupied with those *unpleasant* tasks. I want to be out speaking to groups, visiting schools and prisons, and finding new avenues to share the good teammate message, which is why it's imperative that I adopt the mindset of a sculptor and not a woodcutter.

If I consider the good teammate message to be my masterpiece, I must commit to chipping away at the metaphorical stone that separates me from effectively spreading the message. A dull marketing plan—*a dull chisel*—will make me less efficient. For me, learning about marketing strategies and sales algorithms becomes a way of sharpening my chisel.

Good teammates have the capacity to view unpleasant tasks with a similar perspective. They don't see themselves as sharpening their axe so they can chop more wood. They recognize the importance of paying attention to those elements that make them most effective, while choosing to focus on their deeper purpose. They see themselves as sharpening their chisel so they can help their team create a masterpiece.

As always…Good teammates care. Good teammates share. Good teammates listen. Go be a good teammate.

Critical Instruction
NOVEMBER 5

Two quarterbacks suffered through similar games. Both quarterbacks played poorly. Both got booed by their fans. And both of their teams lost.

Each quarterback, however, responded differently to postgame questions from the media.

When asked about the fans booing him during the game, the first quarterback responded, "I would've booed me to. I wasn't playing up to the standard that our team expects, and our fans deserve better."

When asked the same the question, the second quarterback responded, 'Well I'd like to see one of them come down to the field and try to do better. It's not my fault that passes were dropped or that my line couldn't block or that the right plays weren't called."

The first quarterback took ownership of the issue, conveying class and humility. The second quarterback took it personal, becoming defensive and obsessing over blame.

Their contrasting responses illustrate two completely different approaches to handling criticism. Some choose to handle criticism with grace. Others choose to handle criticism by becoming defensive and deflecting the blame away from themselves. It wouldn't matter what was said to them or by whom it was said, their instinctive reaction will be to bulk at the criticism.

By nature, criticism is difficult to handle. Nobody wants to receive negative feedback, especially when it's delivered in a hurtful manner. Being defensive toward criticism is understandable even if it's labeled as constructive criticism, which is why good teammates choose not to view the feedback as *criticism*.

Good teammates view all feedback—be it negative or positive—as an opportunity to grow. They see feedback as *instruction*.

Good teammates have an innate desire to get better. They are forever searching for ways to improve their individual talents, so they can help their team be successful. A constant desire to improve causes good teammates to crave instruction—the most effective way to create improvement.

Since they choose to view the feedback as instruction instead of criticism, they don't take it personally and they don't mind how it's delivered. Good teammates know that whatever feedback they receive can help them grow.

As I mentioned in last week's blog, many times being a good teammate is nothing more than choosing the appropriate perspective. In this case, it's choosing to accept feedback as instruction instead of criticism.

Criticism hurts. Instruction helps. Everything the second quarterback said in his response may have been true. Receivers may have dropped passes. Linemen may have missed blocks. The wrong plays may have been called. And he may not have been to blame for his poor play.

The same could also apply to the first quarterback. But the first quarterback chose to suppress and not verbalize those thoughts, focusing more on caring about becoming the version of himself that his teammates deserve.

As always…Good teammates care. Good teammates share. Good teammates listen. Go be a good teammate.

Selfishness Awareness
NOVEMBER 12

I was eating breakfast at a McDonald's when I noticed a situation developing outside. The highway department was doing construction on the street in front of the restaurant and had blocked off several lanes with orange cones.

The lane closures were congesting traffic. As cars in the right lane edged forward, they began to block the McDonald's entrance, preventing the cars headed in the opposite direction from turning into its parking lot. Anytime cars in the left lane wanted to enter, they would have to wait on a driver in the right lane to let them across.

Unfortunately, the drivers in the right lane were not allowing cars to cross with any sort of regularity, which led the left lane to become even more backed up. The situation was growing increasingly worse because the cars backed up in the left lane were now blocking the intersection further down the street—preventing the cars in the right lane from turning left.

Because of the orange cones, nobody was able to go around the cars waiting to turn. The situation had grown into a serious traffic jam. Drivers became impatient. They started honking their horns and hurling obscenities—both of which seemed to only exasperate the situation.

As I watched everything develop from inside the McDonald's, I wondered how that many drivers could be so oblivious to their selfishness. Why couldn't they see the problem? The entire situation could be resolved if those in the right lane just left an opening to allow the cars in the left lane to pull into the restaurant.

Too many of the drivers in the right lane were focused on their individual needs to realize the *inconvenience* they were creating for themselves and everybody else. They thought they would get ahead by remaining close to the bumper of the car in front of them but failed to consider the possibility that leaving an opening would actually make them advance faster.

The McDonald's situation epitomizes the problems created by a lack of *selfishness awareness*. Selfishness leads to unnecessary drama on teams. Good teammates have the foresight to appreciate the ramification of their actions. They consciously put themselves in a position to anticipate the inconvenience their decisions could cause the other members of the team.

Awareness of how their actions impact others is a trademark of good teammates. They weigh the inconvenience of others before they act. For example, good teammates would see the need to leave an opening and not block the McDonald's entrance.

Apparently, I wasn't the only one observing the volatile situation developing in front of the McDonald's. It wasn't long until the restaurant's manager had an employee stand near the intersection with a sign that read "Please be kind and don't block the entrance." ("Good teammate move" by the manager!)

The sign worked. Traffic started to flow again. The manager's response was almost perfect. The only way it could have possibly been improved were if he were to have replaced the words "please be kind" with "please be a good teammate." But that may just be a personal preference.

As always…Good teammates care. Good teammates share. Good teammates listen. Go be a good teammate.

Twenty Useful Sports Clichés
NOVEMBER 19

You either love sports clichés or you hate them. I happen to love them. I think sports clichés add to the aura of sports and amplify the excitement of games. I am especially fond of sports clichés that apply to being a good teammate.

Here are twenty classic sports clichés that offer insight into what it means to be a good teammate.

1. "There's no 'I' in team." Good teammates don't have an individual ego, they have a team ego. They base their identity off what their team accomplishes, not in how they looked as an individual player.

2. "They're all heart." Strictly speaking, this isn't entirely true. Good teammates have plenty of physical talent too. But the passion in their heart for their team is clear to anyone who watches them perform.

3. "They're all on the same page." Good teammates commit to the game plan and make a conscious effort to align their beliefs and actions with their team's culture. They refrain from *doing their own thing.*

4. "Throw under the bus." Self-preservation is never a consideration for a good teammate. They don't save themselves by condemning others. However, don't confuse this cliché with confronting a toxic teammate. If something is disrupting the team's culture, good teammates don't hesitate to condemn the toxic behavior.

5. "They're the first one in the building and the last one out." Good teammates are fully invested in their teams. They transform their personal time into "team" time by coming in early and leaving late. That leaves a lot of time in between to make positive strides.

6. "They have unbelievable chemistry." Good teammates sacrifice individual convenience for the betterment of their teams. Because of that, good teammates are able to contort themselves into fulfilling the roles their teams need. Their willingness to sacrifice creates synergy on their team.

7. "They brought their 'A' Game today." Good teammates bring their 'A' Game every day. *Good enough* is never good enough for a good teammate. They're perpetually focused and don't accept anything less than their best. That means they don't coast during drills, take plays off, or save it for the game.

8. "They do all the little things." Good teammates are egoless when it comes to their role. No role is beneath them. Additionally, good teammates pay attention to details. They understand the impact of mastering "the little things."

9. "They do things that don't show up in the stat column." Similar to the previous cliché, good teammates engage in activities that aren't normally measured. With the emergence of advanced metrics, it seems like almost everything is measured in sports today—keyword being *almost*. Experts still haven't come up with a stat for giving high fives, pats on the back, and other general expressions of encouragement that impact team culture.

10. "Their blood, sweat, and tears." This is exactly what good teammates sacrifice for their team. A commitment to serving the needs of their team pours through every pore on their body.

11. "They give 110 percent." They go above and beyond what is expected. While others may be content to meet expectations, good teammates strive to exceed them.

12. "You win as a team, you lose as a team." Good teammates give a consistent effort and maintain a consistent demeanor. They never take individual credit for a win, nor assign blame to someone else for a loss.

13. "They've got ice-water in their veins." Good teammates can be emotional people. But they control their emotions, they don't let their emotions control them. Controlling their emotions precludes them from being rattled during tense moments.

14. "They're students of the game." Good teammates value information. The more knowledgeable they are, the more they are able to contribute. This is why good teammates study the nuances of their craft. But they don't study for themselves, they do it for their team.

15. "They're gym rats." Good teammates love the game. They want to spend every second of their free time working on their skills. They are most comfortable in the gym, in the pool, or on the field. There's no place they would rather be.

16. "They know what it takes to win." Good teammates understand the significance of their commitment to excellence, their ability to effectively execute, and their capacity to espouse enthusiasm—the "things" that lead to victories.

17. "They just want it more." Nobody craves team success more than good teammates. Their desire for their teams to succeed makes them willing to go to lengths that others aren't.

18. "Lions don't roar when they make a kill." A Dean Smith original! Good teammates aren't compelled to boast about individual accomplishments. They handle achievement with humility and grace, as if it's routine.

19. "They're all in." Leaders don't have to worry about the commitment level of good teammates. Good teammates are completely emerged in everything related to their teams.

20. "It doesn't get any better than this." No, it doesn't! Nothing is better than being a part of a team that is comprised entirely of caring, selfless individuals—good teammates.

For the record, I found it difficult to explain many of the above clichés without using clichés. I suppose that *speaks volumes* about their prominence in popular vernacular. *At the end of the day*, I guess *it is what it is*: Good teammates really are *the heart and soul* of their teams.

As always…Good teammates care. Good teammates share. Good teammates listen. Go be a good teammate.

Why Are You Thankful?
NOVEMBER 26

Thanksgiving is a wonderful time for reflection. It's the ideal occasion for us to pause and think about what we're thankful for in our lives.

Some families have a tradition of gathering around the dinner table and stating what each member is thankful for before they eat. (I love this tradition!) Others take to social media to share a list of what they are thankful for. (I love reading these posts!)

Discovering what evokes a sense of gratitude in others is both inspiring and insightful. The discovery offers a glimpse into what others value and a reminder of what we may be taking for granted.

What often gets lost in the practice of sharing gratitude at Thanksgiving, however, is the reason for our thankfulness. We focus on our *what* instead of our *why*. In other words, we tend to state what we're thankful for without explaining why we're thankful.

Assuming others understand why we're thankful for whatever we identified is a mistake that can lead to misinterpretation.

For instance, "our good health" is a common response when asked to name something for which we're thankful. "Our good health" is a worthy response. But it's also the type of response that can be misinterpreted.

Why are you thankful for your good heath? Is it because you don't have to be inconvenienced by illness? Is it because you don't have to bear the financial burdens that accompany treatments? Is it because being healthy gives you the freedom to do whatever you want?

While all those reasons may be true, some could be interpreted as being more selfish than others. Why not take a good teammate approach by removing the doubt and adding some context to your response? Say: "I'm thankful for my good health because it allows me the time and energy to be able to help people I love."

Another common response is for people to be thankful for their family. Again, *why* are you thankful for your family?

Is it because they give you companionship? Is it because they make you laugh? Is because you know they will help you carry boxes the next time you need to move? Or, is it because they give you something to serve and provide purpose in your life?

If you're truly thankful for your family, don't leave them wondering about your reason. Reveal to them the basis for your gratitude. Expressing your thankfulness in this manner provides a deeper understanding of what matters most to you and why it matters.

A few months ago, I wrote a blog about how good teammates state their empathy (*see Chapter 12). Explicitly stating the reasons for your gratitude falls into the same category.

I hope you and your teams have a joyous Thanksgiving, and I hope everyone reading this knows how thankful I am for your continued support. Why? Because every blog you open, every book you buy, every tweet you retweet, and every post you share helps us spread the *be a good teammate* message and makes the world a little bit better place in which to live.

This week, whenever you start spouting off everything you're thankful for remember to also mention *why* you're thankful.

As always…Good teammates care. Good teammates share. Good teammates listen. Go be a good teammate.

32

Playing Out of Position
DECEMBER 3

Of all the unpleasant things I've heard parents utter from the bleachers at youth sporting events, I find one phrase to be the most unsettling: "He/She is playing him/her out of position."

The "he/she" being the coach, and the "him/her" being that parent's child.

I hate hearing parents use this phrase because it reeks of selfishness. The phrase is classic *Me Gear* logic. (Want to know more about this? Read my book *The WE Gear*.) Any parent who thinks this way is unnecessarily setting their child up for future failure.

When parents complain about a coach playing their child out of position, my response is: *So what?*

First, coaches don't make decisions during the season based on what's best for your child. Coaches make decisions based on what's best for your child's *team*. That means your child may be asked to play a position or fulfill a role to which he/she is not ideally suited—for the betterment of the team. The coach's decision is not personal.

Second, parents who blame a coach for playing their child out of position are overlooking an important learning opportunity and a teachable moment. Being asked to sacrifice individual interests for team interests happens all the time on all types of teams. Available personnel and resources dictate the necessity to operate under such confines.

When children enter the workforce, they will be confronted with this reality. How parents approach the issue now will influence how children handle the encounter in their job.

If you, as a parent, approach the issue from the perspective of the coach wronging your child by playing him/her "out of position," you will teach your child to bulk at making personal sacrifices for the good of the team. You will reinforce selfishness and encourage thinking in terms of what's best for them as an individual as opposed to what's best for their team.

Right now, their primary team is their sports team. But eventually, their primary team will be their place of employment, their community, and their family. None of those teams function properly when individual interests are the basis for their members' decisions.

Coaches are human and, if you'll pardon the cliché, sometimes they are so close to the trees that they can't see the forest. Your child may be playing in a position that is not conducive to him/her achieving peak results. But it's a mistake to approach the situation from the perspective of the coach playing your child out of position. Coming at the issue from that angle will force the coach to become defensive and perceive your motives to be self-serving.

Focus instead on what's best for your child's team and you may get a much different response. Approach the situation from the perspective of "I think my child could help the team more if he was to play another position." This simple alteration in perspective could be the difference in your words being received as a vested contribution rather than an unwelcomed critique.

Good teammates take this approach and understand it to be the preferred perspective.

As always...Good teammates care. Good teammates share. Good teammates listen. Go be a good teammate.

Lockdown Logic
DECEMBER 10

Last week, I had an opportunity to attend a freshman English class at a high school where I was speaking. Midway through the class, the principal's voice came over the school's intercom, announcing the commencement of a "lockdown" drill.

I have visited lots of schools and was certainly aware of the existence of these types of drills. My daughters have talked about participating in them at their school and I've seen clips of them on television, but this was the first time I had ever personally experienced a lockdown drill. I found the ordeal to be unsettling.

I think it would be enlightening if others were to experience the drill firsthand.

When the announcement was made, the teacher proceeded to lock the classroom's door and turn off all the lights. The students hustled to find hiding spaces under tables and desks, in closets, and behind cabinets. I wasn't quite sure what I was supposed to do, so I followed their lead and sought a hiding spot in the back corner of the room.

As we hid silently in the dark, I was confronted with a gamut of emotions—anger, sadness, fear, awe, more sadness, and then frustration.

The absurdity of having to practice hiding in the dark angered me, as did the reason for the drill. The exercise seemed inconvenient and a terrible misuse of time. But the more I thought about it, the more I accepted the drill's necessity—which made me sad. We live in a world where school shootings are an unfortunate reality. Training for an active shooter can save just as many lives and is just as prudent as training for fires and tornadoes. This sad reality is scary.

Sitting silently in a dark classroom scared me, as I imagined it also did the students. I knew it was only a drill, but it felt like I was playing a horror movie version of hide-and-seek. The whole situation was unnerving. I was impressed, however, with how the students conducted themselves.

They didn't act scared or annoyed or angered. None of them behaved immaturely. Nobody complained about having to do the drill. They were serious and businesslike. The drill lasted for nearly five minutes and the students remained still and quiet the entire time.

They had clearly been well trained in what to do. After the drill ended, I remarked to the students about how impressed I was with the way they conducted themselves. Several responded that they had been doing lockdown drills since they were in kindergarten. Their matter-of-fact response caused my awe to return to sadness.

It made me sad to think that such an unfathomable reality was routine to them.

When I was leaving the school later that day, a teacher commented that she was glad I came to speak to their students. With such an increased emphasis on testing, the teacher was encouraged to see students exposed to a message that didn't revolve around improving scores.

Of course, the comment frustrated me. The teacher's sentiments are valid. Schools have come to place a premium on test scores and the emphasis on test preparation often eclipses the teaching of important intangibles like kindness, service, and empathy—qualities of good teammates. Many administrations refuse to devote time to anything that doesn't directly impact test scores.

This problem isn't isolated to academia. I see the same misguided logic in the corporate world. Many businesses are too focused on sales goals and financial reports to devote time or resources to anything that doesn't directly impact the "numbers."

In both cases, the entities discount the influence an improved culture can have on productivity. The most prosperous teams—be it sports, business, or other—intentionally make time to work on their culture. That means training team members to practice kindness, service, empathy, etc.

If you don't have time to work on the behaviors that have a positive influence on your culture, when will you find time to resolve the conflicts that result from not doing so?

The great irony is that the teams who make time to work on improving their culture achieve heightened levels of success and waste far less time resolving toxic issues.

The students at the high school I visited told me they typically do a lockdown drill at least once a month. I wonder if the frequency of those drills would still be necessary if schools found ways to devote more time to emphasizing and specifically teaching the aforementioned *intangibles*.

If nothing else, experiencing a lockdown drill reminded me of the significance of the good teammate message. The world needs more *good teammates* now more than ever.

As always...Good teammates care. Good teammates share. Good teammates listen. Go be a good teammate.

Chipless Motivation
DECEMBER 17

Disney has been busy. Last month the company launched their *Disney+* streaming service. This month, they opened *Rise of the Resistance*—the new Star Wars themed ride at Walt Disney World's Hollywood Studios. And this week, they release the much-anticipated final installment of the Star Wars trilogy of trilogies, *The Rise of Skywalker*.

Each of those endeavors involved risk and was accompanied by criticism. But Disney is a company whose foundation is built on risk and the acceptance of inevitable criticism. The origins of this mentality can be traced back to the company's founder and namesake.

Biographers frequently cite the tremendous criticism Walt Disney received for his creative ventures. *Nobody will ever watch a cartoon about a giant mouse. People will never sit through a feature length animated film. That may work on the big screen, but it'll never work on television. You can't build a theme park in the middle of a swamp.*

Walt Disney wasn't deterred by his critics, but he wasn't motivated by them, either. This is one of the most fascinating elements of his career.

So many of us go through life with a proverbial chip on our shoulders. Someone slighted us or doubted our abilities and we use that criticism as our motivation. We become driven to prove our critics wrong.

Walt Disney was an incredibly driven person. However, the source of Walt Disney's drive wasn't proving his critics wrong. He understood that criticism accompanies creativity. Taking risks draws the unavoidable attention of doubters. Walt Disney took risks because he believed them to be necessary. His motivation was the enjoyment of turning his ideas into reality—not proving his critics wrong.

Good teammates operate similarly. The impetus for their actions is never due to slight or doubt. Good teammates don't have, nor need, a chip on their shoulder. They are motivated exclusively by their unquenchable desire to serve the needs of their team.

If taking a risk is the best way to serve their team, then the risk is taken. If making a sacrifice is the best way to serve their team, then the sacrifice is made.

It's worth noting that good teammates don't ignore criticism. They acknowledge and listen to it. Criticism is viewed as feedback and provides them with invaluable insight. To good teammates, criticism isn't a deterrent nor a source of motivation, it's an opportunity to discover how others view their choices.

Being motivated by slight or doubt is as fleeting as being motivated by fear. Individuals who allow themselves to be motivated by a *chip on their shoulder* limit their potential. When you are motivated by purpose, however, your potential is limitless.

Service leads to purpose. Purpose leads to happiness. Happiness leads to being receptive to the sort of inspiration and risk taking that creates the impossible. In the words of Walt Disney, "It's kind of fun to do the impossible."

As always…Good teammates care. Good teammates share. Good teammates listen. Go be a good teammate.

Ten Christmas Movie Good Teammates
DECEMBER 24

Merry Christmas! No deep reading this week, just a fun, lighthearted list to spread a little holiday joy. Here are ten famous Christmas movie good teammates: (*Feel free to debate their merits among yourselves…)

10. Sergeant Al Powell (*Reginald VelJohnson*) *Die Hard*
Whether Die Hard is a Christmas movie may be debatable, but whether Sergeant Al Powell is a good teammate is not. He's loyal and defends John McClane when the FBI and his superiors try to wrongfully vilify Bruce Willis' character. Good teammates don't abandon their teammates during times of peril.

9. Cindy Lou Who (*Taylor Momsen*) *How the Grinch Stole Christmas*
She kept an open mind and didn't allow her thoughts to be swayed by the negative, and more popular, opinions of others.

119

Cindy Lou Who empathized with the Grinch and convinced the citizens of Whoville that the Grinch was simply a misunderstood creature. Good teammates have the courage to stick to their convictions.

8. Clark Griswald, Sr. (*John Randolph*) *Christmas Vacation*
Clark Griswald is a contender for generously welcoming his eccentric relatives into his home, as perhaps is Cousin Eddie for kidnapping Clark's boss. But the best "good teammate" is Clark's father. Good teammates share, and Clark Griswald, Sr. shared his knowledge by teaching his son everything he knows about "exterior illumination."

7. Mother Parker (*Melinda Dillon*) *A Christmas Story*
Not that we need any more evidence than her tolerance of the dreadful leg lamp, but Ralphie's mother was also patient, kind, and caring. She loved her children enough to discipline them. Good teammates hold the other members of their team accountable.

6. Clarence (*Henry Travers*) *It's a Wonderful Life*
Clarence enlightens George to his own obliviousness. Clarence is the angel who helps George see the value he brings to his team. Good teammates believe in others, even when others don't believe in themselves. "Attaboy, Clarence."

5. The Conductor (*Tom Hanks*) *The Polar Express*
The Conductor facilitates hope. He uses his resources to inspire the passengers on his train (team) to believe. Good

teammates are perpetual purveyors of hope. They are the ultimate optimists.

4. Bob Cratchit (*Richard E. Grant*) *A Christmas Carol*

Ebenezer Scrooge's underpaid clerk endures poor working conditions and his boss' abuse. He sacrifices greatly for his family—his *team*. Yet Bob Cratchit selflessly maintains a positive attitude, the way good teammates do.

3. Kevin McCallister (*Macaulay Culkin*) *Home Alone*

Despite being initially scared of his neighbor, Kevin helps "Old Man" Marley reconcile with his estranged son. And...Kevin confronts the threat posed by Marv and Harry. Acting despite fear is a mark of a good teammate.

2. Buddy the Elf (*Will Ferrell*) *Elf*

Buddy makes *good teammate moves*. His enthusiasm is contagious and influences those around him. His commitment to the Christmas spirit is unwavering. Like any good teammate, Buddy is *all in*.

1. Fred Gailey (*John Payne*) *Miracle on 34ᵗʰ Street*

Fred Gailey emerges during Kris Cringle's time of despair. Fred is the lawyer who reassures Kris of his worth and fights for him during his trial. Good teammates stand up for those who cannot stand up for themselves, and Fred Gailey brilliantly stands up for Kris.

As always...Good teammates care. Good teammates share. Good teammates listen. Go be a good teammate and have a merry Christmas!

The Year in Review

DECEMBER 31

We've been fortunate to build a loyal following on social media and have seen that following grow again this year. Our "teammates" enjoy the inspirational thoughts we post each day, and we enjoy sharing the message. Many followers have found our daily posts to be an opportunity to refuel their *good teammate* tanks and discover a rejuvenated purpose in their lives.

If you know of someone who could benefit from a dose of the Good Teammate message, please encourage them to join the conversation and start following us on social media. They can connect with us on the following sites:

Facebook: *https://www.facebook.com/coachloya*
Twitter: *https://twitter.com/coachlanceloya*
LinkedIn: *https://www.linkedin.com/in/coachloya*
Pinterest: *https://www.pinterest.com/coachloya*

As has become our annual tradition, here are the posts from each of the past twelve months that received the most interactions, impressions, shares, likes, favorites, and retweets:

JANUARY

"3 Strategies for Becoming a Better Teammate: 1. Arrive Earlier 2. Work Harder 3. Stay Later."

FEBRUARY

"Good teammates find a way to make those around them better. What are you doing to make your teammates better? #teamwork #sacrifice"

MARCH

"Talk the talk AND walk the walk. Loyalty is substantiated through both words and actions."

APRIL

"Good teammates add light to a dark team."

MAY

"Popularity is temporary. Being a good teammate is timeless."

JUNE

"Good teammates plan thoroughly but remain flexible. Bend but don't break!"

JULY

"When you are wrong, be big enough to own the blame. Good teammates are willing to point their finger at the person in the mirror."

AUGUST

"What does it feel like to be your teammate? Good teammates make others feel appreciated."

SEPTEMBER

"Good teammates understand their choices affect everyone on the team. Consider the ramifications before you speak, act, or fail to act."

OCTOBER

"Block out the gossip and negativity! When the conversation takes a negative tone, good teammates must become tone deaf."

NOVEMBER

"Teamwork doesn't happen without good teammates— individuals who put the team ahead of themselves."

DECEMBER

"The root of a bad teammate always lies in the formation of a clique. Cliques (mini-teams within the main team) destroy teams because they encourage selfishness."

We hope you will continue to support our Good Teammate efforts, as we strive to reach a larger audience and inspire even more individuals to become better teammates. Because the world cannot have too many good teammates. Here's to a prosperous new year!

As always…Good teammates care. Good teammates share. Good teammates listen. Go be a good teammate.

Holding the Flashlight
JANUARY 7

My family had a wonderful Christmas and a happy New Year, but the chaos of the holiday season put our house in a state of wreckage. My daughters were on break from school and seemed to take it upon themselves to play with every toy they owned.

Between the rediscovery of their old toys and the exploration of their new ones, our house looked as if it had been struck by a tornado.

In fairness, my wife and I didn't mind the mess that much. We are aware of the dwindling opportunities we have to watch our daughters play with their toys and we treasure the moments, even if they cause a little messiness. However, we were anticipating company and had reached a point where it was necessary to tidy up our house.

We informed our daughters the cleanup was going to require an "all-hands-on-deck" effort and that everyone on the team (family) was expected to help. A few minutes into the operation, however, I noticed my youngest daughter sitting alone in the corner, playing with a Barbie doll. I told her she wasn't "being a good teammate" and that she needed to help with the cleanup.

She looked at me—with complete sincerity—and said, "I am being a good teammate. I'm staying out of the way and not causing any problems."

I thought about her response for a minute and smiled. Technically, her staying out of our way was allowing us to work faster and not be distracted. Was her staying out of the way a sufficient enough contribution to make her a good teammate?

A lot of individuals think staying out of the way and not causing any problems for others makes them good teammates. But it doesn't. Staying out of the way and not causing any problems may keep them from being bad teammates, but it doesn't make them good teammates.

Good teammates find a way to contribute. They know that the neutrality of non-engagement is an insufficient contribution. Merely staying out of the way is not good enough.

When I was a kid, I used to visit my grandparents. They didn't have cable television at their house. They had an aerial antenna. One evening, the wind blew their antenna loose and my grandfather had to go on the roof to fix it. He told me to get my coat and accompany him.

My grandmother objected, saying I was too small to climb the ladder and not strong enough to turn the antenna. She thought me staying out of the way would be a better option and questioned my grandfather about what possible contribution I could make. My grandfather replied, "He can hold the flashlight."

Every team has its own version of *holding the flashlight*—a small contribution that's better than no contribution. Instead of just staying out of the way and not causing any problems on your team, consider being a better teammate by finding a way to contribute—even if it's as simple as holding the flashlight.

As always…Good teammates care. Good teammates share. Good teammates listen. Go be a good teammate.

Caroline the Compassionate
JANUARY 14

Few of the blogs I write get a more positive response from readers than the features about exceptional service provided by teammates like *Darnell the Mover* (*see Chapter 11, *Teammate Tuesdays Volume I*), *Amy the Balloon Lady* (*see Chapter 33, *Teammate Tuesdays Volume I*), or *The Flying Lullaby* (*see Chapter 1, *Teammate Tuesdays Volume II*). I cross paths with these types of "good teammates" all the time, but it has been a while since I featured one in an edition of *Teammate Tuesdays*.

Saturday, I had an encounter with an employee at Walgreens that's worth sharing.

I was struggling with the store's photo kiosk and couldn't get my order to print. From behind the counter, a friendly employee named Caroline emerged to offer her assistance. Bear in mind, I didn't signal for help or push any help buttons, Caroline noticed me struggling and approached me—and I'm glad she did.

I needed some photos printed for a meeting I had that afternoon and was willing to pay the higher price for the expedited service. Caroline immediately unchecked the expedited option on the screen and selected instead the less expensive one-hour option. I tried to explain to her that I couldn't wait an hour for the photos, I needed them now.

She said the one-hour option would save me some money and that she was going to print my photos right away, so I wouldn't have to wait an hour.

I thought to myself, "Wow! That was nice of her. She didn't have to do that. Caring about saving customers money isn't the typical way business is done."

I waited at the counter while my order printed, and Caroline's smile caught my attention. She had a smile on her face the entire time she worked. Her smile was inspiring. When my photos finished, Caroline brought them to the register. I thanked her for her expediency and for saving me money. She smiled more.

As Caroline tallied up my order, her smile transitioned to a look of concern. I glanced at the total on the register and realized how much she had saved me by changing my order to the less expensive option. I was afraid she had come to the same realization and was worried about getting in trouble with her bosses.

I started to tell her to not worry about the discount. Although I appreciated the gesture, I didn't mind paying the higher price. But before I could get the words out of my mouth, Caroline said, "We can do better than this." She hurried down to the other end of the counter, shuffled through a stack of newspapers, and returned with a coupon.

Caroline scanned the coupon into the register and my total dropped even further.

Some would argue that Caroline was costing her employer money and therefore wasn't being a good teammate. That perspective, however, would be rather shortsighted. After what she just did for me and how she made me feel, do you think there's a chance I will ever choose to get my photos printed from anywhere other than Walgreens? No chance!

Caroline's caring gesture built loyalty with me and I am now happily sharing the positive experience I had with everyone who reads this post. My favorite part of the encounter with Caroline happened after I paid for my photos. I told her the service she provided was too special not to be recognized and asked to take her photo. I've met enough good teammates to not be surprised by her response, yet I still was.

Caroline said, "Oh, you can just fill out the survey on your receipt. Those help our store."

If you've read *The WE Gear*, you already know what I'm going to point out. Caroline wasn't focused on herself. She was thinking about her team. *We can do better than that. Those help **our** store.*

Walgreens has a genuine asset in Caroline. She is exactly the type of compassionate employee—teammate—who makes teamwork happen and why teams succeed. If you've got teammates like her on your team, make sure you value their presence and thank them for what they do.

As always…Good teammates care. Good teammates share. Good teammates listen. Go be a good teammate.

Life Themes
JANUARY 21

Did you make any New Year's resolutions? Are you still committed to them? Or have they already gone by the wayside?

If you've already abandoned your resolutions, you aren't alone. Abandoned New Year's resolutions are a cliché. I heard a statistic on the radio that 50 percent of all resolutions are abandoned by the second week in January and 80 percent are abandoned by the second week in February.

I'm not sure where they got their statistics, but my gut tells me their data is probably right. Keeping New Year's resolutions can be difficult.

An emerging alternative is to adopt a word for the year instead of a resolution. For example, rather than resolving to lose weight choose the word "healthy." This alternative approach works because the word becomes omnipresent and begins to dominate your thoughts. You, in essence, provide a theme to your life, and themes are fun.

The best parties always have a theme (Halloween, Christmas, Harry Potter, Gatsby, etc.). We don't just dress up in costumes for Halloween parties, we eat cookies shaped like ghosts, decorate our house with cobwebs, and play scary music.

Themes provide boundaries and lead us to focus on a specific target, but they also spur creativity and generate enthusiasm. We find ourselves wondering: *How else can I incorporate this theme into what I'm doing?*

What starts as a desire to lose weight turns into an improved diet, increased exercise, decreased stress, and more sleep—all of which contribute to weight loss. Losing weight becomes a byproduct of pursuing "healthy." Before you know it, you're pursuing *healthy* relationships and other *healthy* habits.

Choosing a theme is a proactive approach to steering the direction of your psyche. We are wired to notice patterns and if we aren't careful instead of adopting a theme, a theme will adopt us.

Last year was a challenging year for me. I lost my sister. I lost my father. I even lost my gallbladder. "Losing" could easily become a theme in my life. Allowing that to happen would spur the same creativity and focus to spiral into negativity, as I subconsciously obsess over the *loss* in my life. Choosing a positive theme overshadows the possible negative themes.

Good teammates are deliberate when it comes to choosing the themes in their lives. Words like kindness, compassion, considerate, and unselfish dominate their thoughts.

If your resolutions have already gone by the wayside, know that January 1 is an arbitrary date. You don't have to wait until next year to get back on the wagon or to add a theme to your life. You can add one right now. And if you are looking for a theme, consider the word "teammate."

Most of us belong to multiple teams (place of employment, community, clubs, church, family, etc.). Adding a theme that drives you to become a better teammate on any of your teams will lead to an improved lifestyle and a rejuvenated sense of purpose in your life—and purpose leads to happiness.

As always...Good teammates care. Good teammates share. Good teammates listen. Go be a good teammate.

Paper Towel Problems
JANUARY 28

I have a love/hate relationship with the automatic paper towel dispensers found in public restrooms. I love their convenience. I love their simplicity. I love that there are no handles or levers to touch and therefore no germs to spread. A mere wave of my hand brings forth the paper towel. The process is *almost* Jedi-like.

I hate, however, when the dispensers send forth an inadequate length of paper. Not every dispenser does this, but the ones that do drive me crazy!

I wave my hand under the dispenser's sensor and only a few inches of paper towel come out of the slot. Those few inches aren't nearly enough to sufficiently dry my hands, so I have to wait for the sensor to reset and then repeat the process. The subsequently dispensed amount is still not enough and requires yet another cycle of wait, reset, and repeat.

After three or four cycles, I can finally tear off enough paper towel to dry my hands. But now I'm annoyed and frustrated by the inconvenience of the experience—and so are the people waiting in line behind me.

What frustrates me the most is that the process doesn't have to be this way. Automatic paper towel dispensers come with adjustable settings. Management can choose the length of paper the machines dispense.

I presume the dispensers that are releasing only a few inches at a time are the business' way of saving money. They assume the customer will use less paper if less paper is dispensed, or that maybe the customer won't have the patience to wait through several cycles.

If that is the situation, then their approach is a bit myopic. They are, as the expression goes, being *penny wise but pound foolish.*

The revenues lost through their customers' frustrations outweigh the potential money saved by their customers using less paper. Frustrated customers don't leave happy. Frustrated customers don't spread positive word of mouth. Frustrated customers don't become loyal customers.

I've referenced in the past my fondness of Walt Disney World's standards for customer service (*see Chapter 25, "Keep Your Ears Up," *Teammate Tuesdays Volume II*). They leave no stone unturned in terms of the customer experience, which is why it should come as no surprise that the paper towel dispensers in the restrooms at Walt Disney World are set to release longer towels. A single wave produces a more than adequate length of towel to dry your hands.

The situation with automatic paper towel dispensers is comparable to how some members of a team treat their fellow teammates. Like businesses that use the shorter settings, they don't consider the inefficiency of their actions and the inconvenience they cause the other members of their team. They operate in the *me gear* where self-interest is the basis for their decisions.

Good teammates think about how their choices impact others. They operate in the *we gear* and consider what is best for their team—and causing teammates to be *unnecessarily* inconvenienced, frustrated, or annoyed is never what's best for their team.

Businesses setting their paper towel dispensers to release longer towels is symbolic of how those business view and value their patron's time. Because they demonstrate loyalty and respect for their patrons, the loyalty boomerang inevitably comes back to them. The great irony is that businesses who operate like this end up experiencing sustained success and higher profits.

Their willingness to consider details as seemingly small and insignificant as the length of the paper towels released by their dispensers in their restrooms is indicative of how much they care. Good teammates offer the same level of consideration to details that affect the rest of the team.

As always…Good teammates care. Good teammates share. Good teammates listen. Go be a good teammate.

Walking on Eggshells
FEBRUARY 4

I recently had a client tell me he was tired of "walking on eggshells" around the other members of his team. He felt hampered to express his thoughts and frustrated by what he referred to as his teammates' "fragility."

Isn't *walking on eggshells* a descriptive idiom? It means being deliberately careful and extra sensitive in order to not offend, anger, or hurt someone else. It means being wary of what you say or do and then maneuvering with caution.

When you are part of team, walking on eggshells can become a tiresome practice that forces you to constantly think about what you say before you speak. Every word you choose is vetted for possible offensiveness. Every action you take is weighed and measured. Walking on eggshells is inconvenient, uncomfortable, and not much fun.

The practice makes you feel like you can never drop your guard and be yourself.

My response to the aforementioned client and anyone else who feels this way is this: Maybe the version of *yourself* you want to be isn't the best version of yourself.

Good teammates don't object to walking on eggshells around the other members of their team because they know the practice isn't about them; it's about their teammates.

Walking on eggshells is inconvenient…for *you*. Walking on eggshells is uncomfortable…for *you*. Walking on eggshells is not much fun…for *you*. But being a good teammate isn't about doing what's best for you; it's about doing what's best for your team.

Good teammates accept the necessity of being inconvenienced, taken out of their comfort zone, and sacrificing their fun for the betterment of their team.

While conveying empathy and being sensitive to your teammates' feelings is generally what's best for your team, the necessity to *constantly* walk on eggshells can be a symptom of a dysfunctional team. Don't confuse the practice of walking on eggshells with the acceptance of toxic behaviors or the avoidance of confrontation. The practices aren't exclusive.

You can confront toxicity and still walk on eggshells. Doing so may be inconvenient—for you—but it can be done. Appropriate confrontation requires you to find creative ways to tactfully convey your thoughts and the patience to convey those thoughts at opportune times.

Think of the practice of walking on eggshells as a gift you willingly and freely give to your team.

Bear in mind, however, that your willingness to walk on eggshells does not excuse you to force others to walk on eggshells *with* you. If you find those around you compelled to behave this way, perhaps you should consider adjusting your "fragility" and not being so sensitive.

Making others feel like that they don't have to walk on eggshells around you can be just as impactful of a good teammate move as you not objecting to walking on eggshells around them. How others treat you doesn't have to alter how you treat others.

As always…Good teammates care. Good teammates share. Good teammates listen. Go be a good teammate.

42

Trapped in Your Circle
FEBRUARY 11

I picked up a trinket at an airport gift shop to use as a visual aid in a presentation I made to a group of at-risk youths—a group that traditionally struggles to understand the importance of being surrounded by the right people. Many of these individuals landed in their present predicament because they chose the wrong circle of friends.

I wanted the group to understand how impactful their "circle" can be. As the great Jim Rohn famously pointed out: *We become the average of the five people with whom we spend the most time.* The point I wanted to make to the group was that if they are not careful, their circle of friends can become a trap.

The gift shop trinket had a series of interconnected thin metal rings. When held collapsed, the device looked like a single two-dimensional ring. But a flick of the wrist released the rings and the device expanded to form a three-dimensional sphere that encompassed the person's hand.

I explained to the group that the collapsed ring represented their circle of friends and that the expanded ring represented the influence their circle of friends can have on them. Surrounding themselves with the right people can protect them and provide an opportunity to grow. However, surrounding themselves with the wrong people can trap them into being something they aren't.

The values, morals, and mindset of those around them have a tremendous influence on their standards. Surrounding themselves with the wrong people can limit their ambition and prevent them from becoming the version of themselves they could be.

We all need to periodically remind ourselves of this concept, as it's easy to let the wrong people slide into our circle.

A subsequent point that I made to the at-risk youths may have particular relevance to those of you struggling with the quality of teammates that surround you. I told the group: Sometimes you can't choose the five *people* with whom we spend the most time.

Some of the at-risk youths lived in dysfunctional environments. They had alcoholic parents, drug-addicted siblings, and immoral neighbors. Some were housed in detention centers and surrounded by criminal behavior. Toxic influencers were everywhere.

While you may not be surrounded by those specific types of dysfunction, you may find yourself surrounded by alternative forms of toxicity on your team (selfishness, complaining, complacency, shortsightedness, ego, etc.).

When this is the case, how can you keep your circle from being a trap?

The answer lies in your time. You may not have control over who you have around you, but you have control over how you spend your time. The key is to spend more time around someone who provides a positive influence on you than someone who has a negative influence. The time spent being influenced by a positive source must surpass the time spent being influenced by one of your toxic sources.

You may not be able to find an actual person to fill this role. You may have to replicate the experience by spending your time reading books or watching videos or movies by/about influential persons.

But know that alternative sources of influence are available.

When you flood your time with positive influences, you see a definitive difference in your attitude, values, and mindset. You find yourself caring about what—and who—really matters to you. You become motivated to become a better version of yourself.

As always…Good teammates care. Good teammates share. Good teammates listen. Go be a good teammate.

Declining Reclining
FEBRUARY 18

Isn't it entertaining when a viral video sparks an international debate? Was the dress gold or blue? Did it say Yanny or Laurel? Did he swing toward the building or away from it?

A video of an airline passenger repeatedly hitting the reclined seatback of the passenger in front of him has become the latest source of debate, thrusting the issue of seat reclining etiquette into the pop culture spotlight. Like the other viral videos, the issue has divided viewers.

Some argue that passengers have the right to recline their seat. They paid for their seat and should be able to recline if they choose. Others argue that reclined seats are intrusive to the fellow passengers. Reclined seats prevent people from using the tray or doing work on a laptop computer.

Both sides have valid points, which is why the issue is controversial.

CNN aired a segment yesterday morning where panelists opined about the permissibility of passengers reclining airplane seats. During the segment, panelist Oneika Raymond, from the Travel Channel's *Big City, Little Budget*, made a statement that made me cringe.

Raymond was asked if she was going to think twice about reclining her seat after watching the video. Without hesitation, Raymond responded: "Absolutely not. I don't understand why I should sacrifice my comfort for the comfort of the stranger behind me?"

Her response was tantamount to hearing fingernails scraping a chalkboard. Teams fail when members think like Oneika Raymond. Her response epitomizes *ME gear* logic.

Good teammates—individuals in the *WE gear*—are always considerate of others. They think about how their actions affect those around them and proceed accordingly. Good teammates willingly sacrifice their comfort for the comfort of others.

If the person sitting behind Raymond wasn't a stranger, I wonder if she would still think the same way? What if the person sitting behind her was her grandmother? Her daughter? Her pastor? Would Raymond still be as inclined to recline?

Unfortunately, most of us don't extend the same level of kindness to strangers as we do our friends and family. But the world sure would be a better place if everyone did.

Maybe Raymond's familiarity with the person sitting behind her is inconsequential. Maybe she's so self-centered that she prioritizes her comfort over the comfort of everyone else. Most toxic personalities do.

While I can't condone how the other passenger chose to convey his disapproval of the reclined seat, I find Raymond's justification for reclining the seat to be far more unsettling. *Why should I sacrifice my comfort for the comfort of others?*

Her way of thinking is selfish and unfathomable to a good teammate. Good teammates are kind. They know that kindness comes with a price tag. The price of kindness is the sacrifice of comfort.

When you sacrifice your comfort for the comfort and/or convenience of someone else, you deliver kindness. Your sacrifice becomes a catalyst for success. Teams that are comprised of individuals who *understand* this approach exceed their potential.

As always…Good teammates care. Good teammates share. Good teammates listen. Go be a good teammate.

The Road Less Fair

FEBRUARY 25

Two roads diverged in a yellow wood,
And sorry I could not travel both,
And be one traveler...

I took the one less traveled by,
And that has made all the difference.

If you happen to not recognize those words, they are the opening and closing lines of Robert Frost's famous poem, "The Road Not Taken."

The poem is about life choices and overcoming our natural tendency to choose the more common option. It's about handling uncertainty and the potential consequences of regret. For me, the poem offers an intriguing glimpse into the art of being a good teammate.

A couple of weeks ago, I wrote a blog titled "Walking on Eggshells" (*see Chapter 41). The blog was about the necessity for good teammates to be sensitive with their choice in words and "walk on eggshells" around their fellow teammates, yet not position themselves where others feel compelled to do so around them.

I got an email from a subscriber wondering about the "fairness" of my assessment. He didn't feel is was fair to be expected to walk on eggshells around others and not expect that courtesy to be reciprocated.

He's right. It's not fair. But a lot about choosing to be a good teammate is not fair. It's not fair that you're expected to share, when others on the team are greedy. It's not fair that you're expected to be selfless, when others on the team are selfish. It's not fair that you're expected to confront, when others on the team get away with remaining silent.

Using fairness as a compass is a surefire way to find misery. Your actions shouldn't be dictated by what's fair; they should be motivated by doing what's right. Greed, selfishness, and the avoidance of confrontation are instinctive paths. It's easy to be greedy, selfish, and remain silent.

Similarly when someone hurts you with their words, your instinct may be to retaliate with equally hurtful words. Lowering yourself to their level is the easy choice. The better choice may be to choose the high road.

For good teammates, the road less traveled is usually the high road.

I realize I'm combining clichés and bordering dangerously close to mixing metaphors. But for good teammates, choosing the more ethical option—the high road—is the better choice, even when it's not the fair or most popular option.

Choosing what's best for their team over what's best for them as an individual *is* the expectation of being a good teammate. Choosing to be selfless, courageous, and walk on eggshells is what defines them as a teammate and what makes the difference on their team. Their actions aren't governed by how they are treated, but by how they should treat others.

Much like the narrator in Robert Frost's poem, one day every good teammate will be called to revisit the choices they made in their life—the paths they took—and, much like the narrator, they too will realize the less-traveled paths they chose will have *made all the difference.*

As always...Good teammates care. Good teammates share. Good teammates listen. Go be a good teammate.

Six Phrases Used by Good Teammates
MARCH 3

How we speak reflects how we think. Good teammates are especially effective at conveying their thoughts through their words. Here are six phrases good teammates use:

1. Sincerely, thank you.

Good teammates are appreciative of others. Projecting a clear "attitude of gratitude" is of paramount importance to good teammates. When others know their actions are appreciated, they are far more likely to repeat those actions. Repeated "good teammate moves" are what move the team forward. Good teammates consistently recognize others' "good teammates moves"—with sincerity.

2. The pleasure is mine.

The good folks at Chick-fil-A understand the value of this phrase. Related to the previous point, good teammates appreciate it when *their* "good teammate moves" are recognized. Only good teammates aren't content to respond with the expected "you're welcome." Good teammates let others know that serving is their purpose, and pursuing their purpose is pleasurable.

3. I'm so happy for you.

The only thing that destroys a team quicker than apathy is jealousy. Apathy keeps team members from acting, but jealousy motivates team members to engage in destructive action. Good teammates are never jealous of the achievements of other team members. Good teammates understand that when one team member achieves, the entire team achieves. To ward off jealousy, express your happiness for teammates' achievements.

4. I'm proud to be your teammate.

While good teammates value character over reputation, they realize that being part of a team means their reputation is affected by the actions of the other members of the team. Whenever someone on the team does something that reflects positively on the entire team, good teammates feel a sense of pride. They let that person know they are proud to be their teammate.

5. You're making a difference.

Making sacrifices for the betterment of the team can be both physically and emotionally taxing. Good teammates remind others that their sacrifices are not in vain. Being reminded that prioritizing the needs of the team over self-interests validates sacrifices and discourages regret. Let your teammates know their sacrifices and their actions are making a difference.

6. Don't stop.

We all need encouragement, especially when the fruits of our labor are slow to materialize. Uttering these two simple words—*don't stop*—can be the difference between teammates failing or succeeding. Encouraging a teammate who is struggling influences the path of your team's journey. It's not enough for you to be filled with determination. To be a good teammate, you need to encourage those around you to also be determined. (And if you've got a good teammate on your team, tell them: "Don't ever stop being *you*.")

As always...Good teammates care. Good teammates share. Good teammates listen. Go be a good teammate.

Silly Canned Yoda
MARCH 10

My daughter and her friends were giggling and having fun in the backseat of our car. They're tweens and listening to them being kids and enjoying life is one of my life's greatest joys.

As we cruised down the highway, my daughter shouted to the front of the car, "Dad, can you play the *Silly Canned Yoda* song?"

Silly Canned Yoda? I had no idea what song she wanted and judging by the looks on her friends' faces, neither did they. My daughter proceeded to hum a few notes and then belted out (in earnest): "Like the Silly Canned Yoda." The car erupted in laughter, as we all instantly realized she was referring to Macklemore's "(Ceiling) Can't Hold Us."

I laughed. My wife laughed. My daughter's friends laughed. But perhaps most significantly, my daughter laughed—at herself.

Exposing our belief in misheard lyrics can be an embarrassing experience, especially when we seem to be the only one who believed that was the actual lyric. How we respond to the revelation that we had subscribed to a false belief can be insightful.

Every successful team has an occasional *Silly Canned Yoda*—a lighthearted moment that reminds everyone that we're all human and therefore vulnerable to missteps. We should never allow our egos to get too big to laugh at our missteps.

Successful teams have *Silly Canned Yoda* moments because they're comprised of good teammates, and good teammates don't take themselves too seriously. They work hard. They're serious about the direction of their team and about being a good teammate, but they remain able to laugh at themselves.

A telltale sign of a toxic teammate is an inability to laugh at himself or herself.

The ability to laugh at oneself factors into healthy relationships. Research from a Cal-Berkeley study done a few years ago showed the ability to laugh at oneself to be distinct character trait, linked to having an upbeat personality and an eternally good mood—two attributes of good teammates.

Laughter is a powerful emotion, capable of bonding teams. Situations that illicit laughter offer an opportunity to experience shared emotion. We tend to remember positive emotions we experienced with our teammates with fondness.

Laughter is also an incredibly contagious emotion. While I, my wife, and my daughter's friends laughed at my daughter's mistaken song title, so did my mother-in-law. And my mother-in-law didn't even know that song! She didn't recognize my daughter's mistake. She laughed at us laughing—a statement on the irresistibility of laughter.

The next time you experience a *Silly Canned Yoda* moment, be humble enough to laugh at yourself. The experience could be the bonding opportunity your team needs.

By the way, good luck getting "Silly Canned Yoda" out of your head. It's hard to un-hear. Macklemore's song will never be the same for you. If I gave you an earworm, my apologies. If I gave you a laugh, you're welcome.

As always…Good teammates care. Good teammates share. Good teammates listen. Go be a good teammate.

*The Cal-Berkeley study referenced is from Ursula Beermann and Willibald Ruch, "Can People Really 'Laugh at Themselves?'—Experimental and Correlational Evidence," American Psychological Association, Emotion (2011), Vol. 11, No. 3, 492–501.

47

The Wearin' of the Green
MARCH 17

Happy St. Patrick's Day! Will you be *wearin' the green* today? Will you down any shamrock shakes or green beer? Will you eat corned beef and cabbage?

St. Patrick's Day is a fun, festive holiday. I've come across people who don't like Valentine's Day. I've encountered people who scoff at Groundhog Day. I've even known a few people who hate Christmas. But I don't know anyone who doesn't enjoy celebrating St. Patrick's Day.

The Irish have recognized March 17th as St. Patrick's Day since the early 1600s. The date commemorates the anniversary of the death of the holiday's namesake, a missionary credited with bringing Christianity to the Emerald Isle.

Interestingly, green was not the color originally associated with St. Patrick's Day. Blue was. The Knights of the Order of St. Patrick wore a lighter shade of blue known as "St. Patrick blue." Green didn't become connected to the holiday until the Irish rebellion in 1798.

The Irish sought independence from British rule and began wearing shamrocks (clovers) on their lapels and in their hats as a symbol of Irish unity. The movement grew to include wearing green capes and green uniforms. The British eventually deemed wearing green as a rebellious act, punishable by death.

A popular folk song of the time, "The Wearin' of the Green," mocked the much-detested law and became the battle cry for Irish nationalism. The song's theme captures an important aspect of being a good teammate: *fearless loyalty*. Take notice of the song's final verse:

> *When laws can stop the blades of grass from growin' as they grow*
>
> *And when the leaves in summer-time their color dare not show*
>
> *Then I will change the color too I wear in my caubeen*
>
> *But till that day, please God, I'll stick to the Wearin' of the Green.*

When will laws stop grass from growing? Never. When will summer-time leaves stop being green? Never. When will the narrator stop wearing shamrocks in his hat? Never. When will fear keep a good teammate from being loyal? Never.

Good teammates have an unwavering commitment to their team. They don't jump ship when the seas get rough.

They don't quit when the demands are high. And they don't let the opinions of outsiders scare them into diminished support for their team. Good teammates are *all in*.

An emphasis on individuality monopolizes our society. People are always trying to set themselves apart to the extent that uniformity is practically spurned. Good teammates value individuality, but they also embrace uniformity. Good teammates seek individual identity through team uniformity.

For all the negative talk surrounding the state of professional sports, the NFL, NBA, MLB, NHL, and MLS still value uniformity. All those organizations enforce strict rules for how players dress. They regulate everything from how uniforms are worn to the type of socks players can use. A big part of professional sports' success is the pride taken in their product's uniformity.

If professional athletes want to pursue individuality on the field or court, they must do so within the confines of the league's rules for uniforms.

Good teammates take pride in practicing uniformity and in being part of their team. If you're *wearin' the green* today, wear it with pride. Embrace the spirit of St. Patrick's Day with the fearless loyalty of a good teammate.

As always…Good teammates care. Good teammates share. Good teammates listen. Go be a good teammate.

48

Overcoming Cabin Fever
MARCH 24

The COVID-19 situation sure has thrust the world into uncharted territory. Every time I think the situation can't get any more surreal, it somehow does.

Like many of you, my family is doing our best to navigate the challenges of social distancing and home quarantine. I regrettably acknowledge that the memes about home schooling that I laughed at last week aren't nearly as funny this week. Trying to work from home while overseeing my daughters' schoolwork has not been easy!

During times of uncertainly, it's natural to draw upon our past experiences for guidance in handling our present predicament. While the COVID-19 situation is new to me, I have experienced the challenges of isolation and dealing with cabin fever before.

When I was a student-athlete, our college would shut down during the semester break. Because our season overlapped both semesters, my teammates and I were usually the only students on campus. If that weren't enough of a challenge, our campus was in the northeastern United States. Winter snowstorms and freezing temperatures usually prevented us from leaving the dormitory.

Being around the same people in such limited quarters for that length of time made me appreciate the truth in the expression *familiarity breeds contempt.*

Certain players on our team were better at handling the confinement than others. Some players were overtaken with cabin fever and seemed to be constantly entangled in conflict with somebody else on the team. But the "good teammates" never were.

I witnessed the same phenomenon when I coached teams that were confined to the dorms over the semester break. I spent a lot of my coaching career resolving the cabin fever conflicts that occurred during the course of those weeks.

I felt the good teammates in both situations adhered to three simple practices that made their confinement much more tolerable:

1. They all had a "safe place" where they retreated to escape the monotony. When someone was getting on their nerves, they found refuge in their solitude. Sometimes their safe place was the bathroom. Other times is was putting their headphones on and lying quietly on their bed.

They always found a particular spot to escape from what was annoying them. They also respected when their teammates sought seclusion. The good teammates refused to bother team members who retreated to places of solitude. Safe places were sacred to good teammates.

2. They never projected their pleasures on another teammate. So many of the conflicts I dealt with as a coach revolved around one player not liking another player's loud music, or one player not liking the smell of the food another player was heating up in the microwave. If not managed, those trivial conflicts would quickly escalate. When people are confined to tight quarters, annoying habits become amplified.

The good teammates listened to their music on their headphones so they wouldn't disturb anyone else. They avoided eating smelly foods and were otherwise considerate of those around them. They sacrificed the pleasures of "me" for the benefit of "we."

3. They adopted a routine. Quite often, the good teammates steered clear of conflicts by just sticking to a routine. They got up at a consistent time. They ate at a consistent time. They showered at a consistent time. And they went to bed a consistent time.

When people get bored, they become irritable. The same is true when people get hungry or tired. An unhealthy diet— like snacking on junk food—can make you more susceptible to mood swings and so can disrupted sleep patterns. By sticking to a routine, the good teammates limited their moodiness and made themselves more pleasant to be around.

For many of us, the phrase "March Madness" has taken on an entirely different meaning. I hope sharing these three tips will help make the *madness* of your home confinement more tolerable.

As always...Good teammates care. Good teammates share. Good teammates listen. Go be a good teammate.

Get Rid of It
MARCH 31

On more than a few occasions lately, I've caught myself standing in the middle of our kitchen, pondering the totality of the COVID-19 pandemic. The uncertainty of how much longer it will be until our lives return to normal is hard to digest.

As I lapsed into my thoughts this morning, I happened to glance up and notice my wife's tin collection. She has dozens of Hershey's Chocolate tins on display on the top of our kitchen cabinets. She's been collecting them since she was in middle school.

I pass through our kitchen several times every day, and rarely do I even notice these tins anymore. They usually blend into the background like wallpaper. But this morning, the tins caught my eye. They reminded me of one of my favorite "good teammate" stories.

During the Great Depression, Milton S. Hershey—the founder of the Hershey's Chocolate Company—used his fortune to create jobs and keep the residents of his town from suffering the same economic hardships as the rest of the country. Most of the jobs he created stemmed from the multiple building projects his company had initiated, despite having no need for expansion.

The projects weren't part of a strategy to pursue growth amid an opportune juncture. Expansion of any kind was financially ill-advised. Hershey took on the projects for the sole purpose of creating jobs for his townspeople.

Among the building projects launched during this period was the luxurious Hotel Hershey. My wife and I stayed at this hotel a few years ago. It was a chocoholic's paradise. The staff placed Hershey Kisses on guests' pillows at night. A chocolate aroma permeated the hotel's hallways. The featured channel on the rooms' televisions looped a Hershey's history documentary.

A story in the documentary about Milton S. Hershey visiting the hotel's construction site left an impression on me. While standing on a hill overlooking the project, a foreman pointed out to Hershey a new mechanical wonder known as a "steam shovel." The foreman told Hershey the machine was able to do the work of forty men.

Though impressed with the machine, Hershey promptly replied with explicit instructions for the foreman to *get rid of it* and hire forty men.

Hershey's construction projects weren't about efficiency or profit margins. The projects were about jobs. They were about taking care of his people—his *teammates*.

I share this story because I know there are leaders and persons of influence who read this blog. The best leaders always see themselves as part of the team. They might have a different role than others on the team, but they must still be committed to having the mindset of a good teammate (care, share, and listen). Milton S. Hershey exemplified this concept.

The COVID-19 pandemic and the necessity for social distancing will eventually pass. But the economic hardships caused by the quarantine will probably linger long after their passage. If that is to be the case, may Hershey's example inspire us all to serve our fellow teammates and adopt a *get-rid-of-it-and-hire-forty-men* mentality.

As always…Good teammates care. Good teammates share. Good teammates listen. Go be a good teammate.

Crisis Mode Teammates
APRIL 7

Isn't it amazing how tragedy can bring out the best in people? I think it's one of life's greatest ironies. Life's worst elicits humanity's best. People kick into "crisis mode" and exhibit extraordinary levels of kindness and generosity.

We've seen plenty of examples of this during the COVID-19 pandemic: businessmen donating their private planes to transport supplies and essential personnel, companies reconfiguring their factories to produce medical supplies, landlords suspending the rent of furloughed workers, students creating homemade face masks for nursing homes, and so forth.

I make a point to share every story of this nature I see on social media and comment, "Good teammate move!" Selfless acts of kindness cannot receive too much attention.

Crisis mode has a unique way of *rallying the troops*—at least in the beginning. But as the crisis drags on, the heightened levels of kindness, generosity, patience, and commitment inevitably wane.

I've written before about how remarkable everyone's behavior was on September 12, 2001 (*see Chapter 20, "When Tragedy Leads to Good Teammates," *Teammate Tuesdays Volume II*). People seemed a lot more patient than usual that day. Unfortunately, people weren't nearly as kind and patient on October 12, 2001.

We see this same situation play out in the sports world. A team's season will get off to a rocky start. They lose a few close games in the beginning of the year and everybody on the team shifts into crisis mode. Everybody is willing to do "whatever it takes" to find success. Overcoming the losses becomes an "all-hands-on-deck" affair.

But then the team loses a few more games. And then a few more. As the losing streak lengthens, the commitment of those team members who vowed to do "whatever it takes" gradually fades. People shift back into the *me gear* and begin prioritizing their individual interests over those of the team.

If void of a true commitment, crisis mode can turn out to be little more than a flash in the pan. The virtues that initially accompanied crisis mode become a fad. Good teammates don't have a crisis mode. They are eternally kind and patient—and committed.

When a team finishes a season 3-15 but then turns it around the next season to go 15-3, without any influx of new talent or leadership, we wonder how they did it. The answer is quite simple: Their team was comprised of *good teammates* who had faith, believed in the process, and were committed to solving the problem. They stuck with it and kept grinding.

Crises test our resolve and our resilience. But more than anything, crises test our commitment to winning principles and winning methods.

When you feel your faith and commitment waning, ask yourself: *Do I want to be a good teammate?* If you do, then get back in the saddle and forge ahead with the belief that something good is coming.

I wish I had the space to list every example of the good teammate moves I've heard about during the COVID-19 pandemic. They are all worthy of recognition. If you hear of a good teammate move story, be sure to offer praise and share the news with others. These stories inspire us and refuel our spirit.

As always...Good teammates care. Good teammates share. Good teammates listen. Go be a good teammate.

Worth the Grief
APRIL 14

I recently shared a quote about grief on my social media pages. The quote is credited to Sophocles, the Greek playwright who wrote *Oedipius Rex* and *Antigone*.

"The greatest griefs are those we cause ourselves."

Sophocles is believed to have written over 120 plays, but only seven have survived in complete form. The fifth century B.C. playwright is known for his tragedies. While the above quote carries tragic overtones, it—ironically—also contains the path to one of life's greatest sources of happiness.

In *The WE Gear*, I describe the ability to differentiate between chasing pleasure and pursuing happiness as a defining characteristic of a good teammate. Good teammates pursue happiness. They don't chase pleasure.

My interest in understanding how to better pursue happiness has led me to become a fan of author Gretchen

Rubin. Her field of expertise is happiness. A few months ago, I completed Rubin's online course, The Happiness Project Experience. I am fascinated by a concept she discusses in the June module about the three categories of fun— *challenging, accommodating,* and *relaxing.*

Challenging fun is taking up a new hobby or learning a new skill. This type of fun takes patience and perseverance— and usually a considerable amount of time and energy.

Accommodating fun would be attending an office party, taking a family trip, or going out to dinner with a group of friends. Accommodating fun necessitates coordination, organization, inconvenience, and some "give and take" on your part.

Relaxing fun entails virtually no effort. It's watching television, scrolling through Facebook posts, and chilling by the pool.

Most of our "fun" time is occupied by relaxing fun. However, challenging fun and accommodating fun tend to bring us more happiness and produce the best memories. Why is this?

Because, relaxing fun involves little effort. Challenging fun and accommodating fun compel a greater commitment. Putting forth more effort strengthens our bond to the experience. To paraphrase Gretchen Rubin: *We get more out of it because we put more into it.*

Being a good teammate requires sacrifice, concessions, inconvenience, ambition, and love—all potential sources of grief *and* all brought on by our own choice. Helping a wayward teammate find the right path can cause you a lot of grief. But much like the sources of challenging and accommodating fun, helping your teammate can leave you with the best memories and highest levels of happiness.

Few endeavors will bring you more happiness than being the reason a teammate who falls down seven times, stands up eight. The happiness brought on by this struggle will be worth the grief. The greatest griefs can indeed bring us the greatest happiness.

As always…Good teammates care. Good teammates share. Good teammates listen. Go be a good teammate.

Miss Cici, "The Bookend Teammate"
APRIL 21

The expression *absence makes the heart grow fonder* holds enormous truth—the longer we are away, the more we yearn. *Absence makes the heart grow fonder* is the yin to *familiarity breeds contempt*'s yang.

While being confined in the same place with the same people during the COVID-19 quarantine may be testing your resolve, I suspect it may also be creating distance in your life that leaves you yearning for what is absent.

Is it dining out at your favorite restaurant? Attending sporting events? Your morning commute? Your coworkers? Distance facilitates our ability to gloss over the bad and amplify the good. Distance also facilitates our appreciation for things that we didn't necessarily realize we appreciated—until they were gone.

I find myself increasingly missing things that fall into this category, like the crossing guard at my daughter's school, Miss Cici.

Before the quarantine, I walked my daughters to school every morning. Miss Cici brought a unique brand of flare and enthusiasm to the intersection in front of their school. She didn't just blow her whistle and raise her stop sign when it was time for the students to cross the street. Miss Cici tooted her whistle in a zealous cadence before shouting, "Loooooooook and gooooooo!"

When it was time to stop crossing, she didn't just drop her stop sign and return to the curb, she counted down from ten before declaring in her patented, *sing-songy* tone: "No more crossing, Pleeeeeeeaaaase waaaaaaaaaaaaiiiite." Of course, intermingled between crossings were plenty of *goooooooood morning's*, *greeeeeeaat to see you's*, and *have a niiiiiiiiice day's*.

Miss Cici's style gained the attention of everyone who approached the intersection. You couldn't help but smile when you passed through her crosswalk.

To the students and parents at my daughter's school, Miss Cici is a bonafide good teammate. But she's a special type of good teammate, she's a *bookend teammate*. Her welcoming disposition set the tone for everyone's day, and her enthusiasm sent us home with gladness and an eagerness to return.

All great teams have bookend teammates—individuals who greet team members with enthusiasm and send team members off with an eagerness to return. Bookend teammates play an integral part in team culture because they set the tone and *reset* the tone.

Businesses with high customer satisfaction ratings always have bookend teammates. They are found in roles like receptionist, doorman, and hostess. Bookend teammates influence the mood of the patrons entering the business and the quality of the patrons' experience when exiting. Wise leaders—leaders who see themselves as needing to also be good teammates—value their teams' bookend teammates.

With the growing trend towards Kindles and eBooks, the bookend analogy may not translate as smoothly as it once did. To those unfamiliar with the term, bookends are structures used to keep a group of loose books together on a shelf. They keep the books from falling apart.

Metaphorically, bookend teammates serve the same purpose to their teams.

Being a bookend teammate requires no special talent. All that's really needed is a willingness to share their enthusiasm and appreciate the importance of their role. I suppose that's true for all good teammates.

As always…Good teammates care. Good teammates share. Good teammates listen. Go be a good teammate.

Bring the Good Teammate
Message to Your Team

Are you interested in bringing the "Good Teammate" message to your event or implementing strategies to improve the quality of the teammates you have on your team? If so, contact Lance Loya at:

Phone: (814) 659-9605

E-mail: info@coachloya.com

Website: www.coachloya.com

Twitter: @coachlanceloya

Facebook: facebook.com/coachloya

LinkedIn: linkedin.com/in/coachloya

Join the movement and sign up for Lance Loya's weekly *Teammate Tuesday* blog at *www.coachloya.com/blog*.

*If you have enjoyed this book or it has inspired you in some way, we would love to hear from you! Be a good teammate and share your photos and stories with us through email or social media. We want to hear from you!

About the Author

Lance Loya is the CEO and founder of The Good Teammate Factory. He specializes in getting individuals to shift their focus from *me* to *we* and discover genuine purpose in their lives. Lance previously wrote the children's book *Be a Good Teammate* and the adult nonfiction titles *Building Good Teammates: The Story of My Mount Rushmore, a Coaching Epiphany, and That Nun*; *Teammate Tuesdays: A Year of Good Teammate Musings*; *Teammate Tuesdays Volume II: Another Year of Good Teammate Musings*, and *The WE Gear: How Good Teammates Shift from Me to We*.

A college basketball coach turned author, blogger, and professional speaker, he is known for his enthusiastic personality and his passion for turning *teambusters* into good teammates. He has inspired readers and audiences around the globe through his books, keynotes, and seminars.

When not speaking or writing, he is a loyal husband to his high school sweetheart and a doting father to his two daughters—who, incidentally, were the impetus behind his heartwarming children's book.

Also by Lance Loya

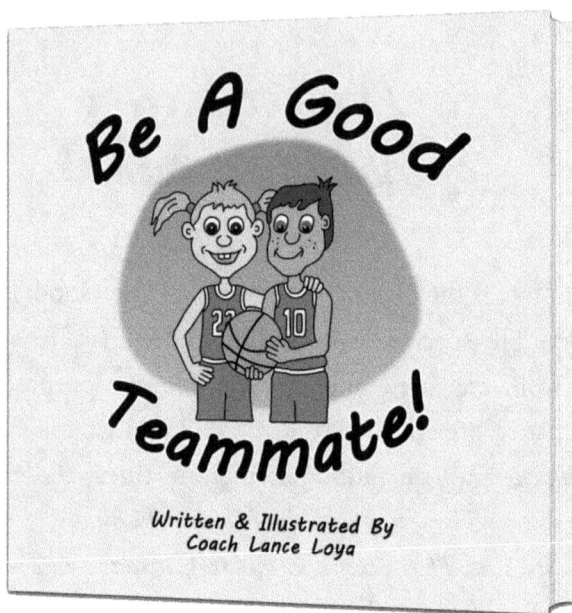

Be A Good Teammate!

Written & Illustrated By
Coach Lance Loya

Be a Good Teammate is an illustrated children's book that teaches kids the importance of teamwork and the three undisputable characteristics of all good teammates. Good teammates care. Good teammates share. Good teammates listen. You don't have to play sports to be on a team. Everybody is part of a team in some capacity! This book encourages kindness and counters bullying.

WWW.COACHLOYA.COM

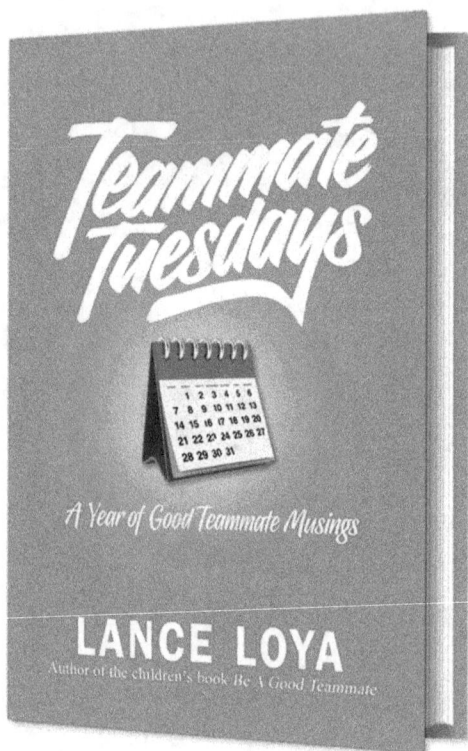

Also by Lance Loya

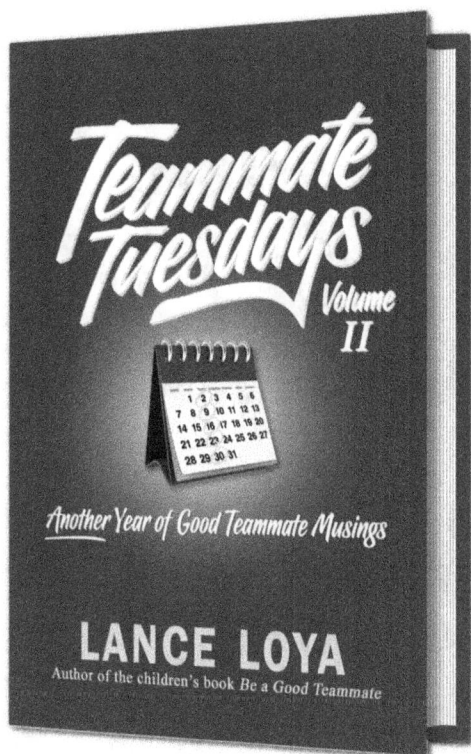

Teammate Tuesdays: Volume II is the compilation of the second year of Lance Loya's popular weekly blog of the same name. This edition contains fifty-two more *musings* about the art of being a good teammate. Topics include ideas for improving teamwork, communication, and empathy on teams. The book also has inspiring stories that are guaranteed to make readers want to become better teammates.

WWW.COACHLOYA.COM